YAS

DO ANIMALS HAVE RIGHTS?

Jamuna Carroll, *Book Editor*

Bruce Glassman, *Vice President*
Bonnie Szumski, *Publisher*
Helen Cothran, *Managing Editor*

GREENHAVEN PRESS
An imprint of Thomson Gale, a part of The Thomson Corporation

D1213649

Detroit • New York • San Francisco • San Diego • New Haven, Conn.
Waterville, Maine • London • Munich

© 2005 Thomson Gale, a part of the Thomson Corporation.

Thomson and Star Logo are trademarks and Gale and Greenhaven Press are registered trademarks used herein under license.

For more information, contact
Greenhaven Press
27500 Drake Rd.
Farmington Hills, MI 48331-3535
Or you can visit our Internet site at http://www.gale.com

LIBRARY OF CONGRESS CATALOGING-IN-PUBLICATION DATA

Do animals have rights? / Jamuna Carroll, book editor.
    p. cm. — (At issue)
  Includes bibliographical references and index.
  ISBN 0-7377-2332-7 (lib. bdg. : alk. paper) —
  ISBN 0-7377-2333-5 (pbk. : alk. paper)
    1. Animal rights. 2. Animal rights—Moral and ethical aspects. I. Carroll, Jamuna. II. At issue (San Diego, Calif.)
  HV4708.D56 2005
  179'.3—dc22
                                                                2004042519

Printed in the United States of America

Contents

Introduction

For decades, the question "Do animals have rights?" has been examined from many different angles. People contend that animals do or do not have rights based on several factors, including whether animals can learn, can use language, are conscious, are able to suffer, and are ethical beings. Whether and which animals have rights depends on which characteristics are considered.

Some say that the only animals with rights are those that can learn and rationalize. In this light, many species are denied rights, including bugs, birds, and reptiles. Under this premise, however, great apes (chimpanzees, orangutans, bonobos, and gorillas) would be granted rights. Proof of their intelligence lies in documentation that they use and make tools, live in complex societies, treat illnesses with medicinal plants, and can add fractions. Indeed, the international Great Ape Project contends that due to their humanlike abilities, great apes deserve the same rights to life and liberty that humans enjoy. Rats and mice, too, as seen in experiments that offer rewards for efficiently completing a maze, can learn. However, many analysts contend that deciding whether or not a particular animal has rights goes beyond determining its intelligence; for these commentators, an animal's ability to communicate should be considered in deciding whether to grant it rights.

Many rights advocates say animals that are competent in human language ought to have rights. For more than thirty years, researchers have studied the ability of great apes to use sign language. A gorilla named Koko is said to have a vocabulary of over one thousand signs. She understands two thousand spoken words and often invents signs for words she has not been taught. However, in "The Soul of the Ape," Clive D.L. Wynne summarizes the results of one chimpanzee study, which he says are not uncommon:

> The animal's vocabulary developed painfully slowly, and it never exceeded a couple of hundred signs (about two weeks' work for a healthy two-year-old child). Often the chimp involved could only repeat gestures, and in any case, chimpanzee "sentences" rarely extend beyond one or two signs.

Moreover, he claims, instances in which a great ape forms a new combination of signs for a word it has not been taught, such as signing "water" and "bird" for swan, are rare and do not necessarily indicate a capacity for language. Instead, the animal may be signing for two things it sees, water and bird. In this view, advanced animals can imitate signs but cannot truly understand communication like humans do.

Philosopher René Descartes deduced that no animals have rights because they do not use language, and because, he asserted, they are not conscious. Loosely defined, consciousness is a state of being aware, especially of oneself, that may be characterized by emotion and thought. Sometimes referred to as sentience, it is important in the animal rights debate, says animal rights lawyer Steven M. Wise, "because species with no capacity for it lack that quality of mind that matters for legal rights. They're not aware that they, or anyone else, exist. . . . Entitlement to legal rights rests upon the existence of conscious states." He notes that some animals, like great apes, behave in a way that suggests similar mental processes to ours. For instance, he contends that apes understand cause and effect, they deceive and empathize with others, and they recognize themselves in mirrors (by noticing a splash of dye on their faces, for example).

Wynne disagrees. Simply because great apes can recognize themselves in mirrors does not prove self-awareness, he points out. He cites blind people who cannot see themselves but are clearly self-aware, and autistic children whose self-awareness is clearly impaired but who can still recognize their reflections.

This raises the question of whether animals can have conscious minds without sharing all the attributes, such as self-awareness or emotion, of human consciousness. Animal behaviorist Marian Stamp Dawkins says, "Different animals might possess some or all of these attributes to different extents, so that it may not be possible to say that an animal is either conscious (possessing all elements) or not (possessing none)." With consciousness seen as a spectrum, less complicated animals might experience dreamy, incoherent consciousness, while deeply conscious creatures think complex thoughts and experience highly sophisticated feelings.

Still, some argue that consciousness is not a strong enough attribute upon which to base animal rights. Philosopher David S. Oderberg states that even if animals are sentient,

> The truth is that there is no straight entailment between consciousness . . . and the possession of rights. What is the logical connection between sentience and rights? Feeling pain/pleasure is just another way that a creature's life can go badly/well for it. . . . So why don't plants have rights? They aren't sentient, but their lives can go well or badly in other ways.

Descartes saw both plants and animals as lacking consciousness, so, he surmised, they are aware of neither pleasure nor pain. Therefore, he writes, animals are mere "automatons or moving machines." In fact, when Descartes and his followers performed experiments in which they burned and mutilated animals, he claimed the animals' whines were no different from the sounds of a machine that was malfunctioning or a gear that needed oil. Unable to feel pain, these creatures need not be shielded by humans, he reasoned.

Many disagree with this conclusion. Animals' ability to feel pain, says philosopher Jeremy Bentham, is the only factor that should be considered in weighing whether animals matter morally. He writes, "The question is not, Can they *reason?* nor, Can they *talk?* but, Can they *suffer?*" Similarly, civil rights attorney William Kunstler contends, "Pain is pain, irrespective of the race, sex, or species of the victim." Rights advocates point out that many animals are used in research into human pain and pain relieving drugs. In experiments in which animals self-administer analgesics after surgery, mice and rats are chosen as test subjects because they perceive physical pain that is comparable to that of humans. Birds also feel pain, as evidenced in studies that measure how fast birds jump as their feet touch a hot plate.

Gary L. Francione takes Bentham's argument one step further, claiming that animals have *interests* in not experiencing pain. Animal welfare laws were designed to prohibit humans from inflicting unnecessary suffering on animals, but fall short of the mark, he says. In *Introduction to Animal Rights: Your Child or the Dog?*, he speaks of the importance of balancing animal interests and human interests:

> If the balance tips in favor of humans—if human interests in inflicting harm on an animal are stronger than the animals' interests in not being made to suffer—we consider that the use or treatment is morally justified because it is necessary. . . . We *must* agree that if the prohibition against animal suffering is to have any meaning at all, it is morally and legally wrong to inflict suffering on animals merely for our amusement.

Perhaps the most important discussion in the animal rights debate revolves around whether animals are ethical creatures. In the *Journal of Evolutionary Psychology*, Stanley M. Giannet writes, "Scientists claim that the cardinal difference between animals and humans is that humans have a capacity for moral judgments and thought. We are ethical sentient beings whereas animals are only sentient beings." By this he refers to assertions that humans can weigh moral aspects in making decisions while animals cannot. For example, in determining whether to shoot a bear that is pregnant or has young cubs in tow, a hunter can consider ethical reasons not to kill it, such as the bear's responsibility to its cubs. Animals, on the other hand, have no regard to the lives, responsibilities, or feelings of other living things, as is the case when a bear attacks and kills a person whose family is nearby.

Writer and philosopher Roger Scruton frames the issue this way: "American jurisprudence has always been clear that rights cannot be had for free. . . . Rights cannot be invented without also inventing the social and legal relations that enable us to uphold them. . . . Rights ought not to be given but purchased, and the price is duty."

Charles R. Pulver, who writes for the Catholic weekly *Wanderer*, offers an illustration. If an eagle has a legal right to life, it would be bound to respect the same rights granted to a mouse. Once the eagle eats a mouse, the eagle would have to be convicted and punished for committing murder. Pulver writes,

> The majestic bird must be read his Miranda rights, be given counsel, and be tried by a jury of his peers. We may assume that his "peers" should be members of his own species, i.e., fellow eagles. Or perhaps mice should be included on the jury, since eagles would be strongly biased to favor the defendant. . . . Would the convicted killer get life without parole or the death penalty?

Illustrating "the utter foolishness of so-called animal rights," Pulver concludes that animals can never hold duties because they cannot distin-

guish right from wrong and have no moral sense as humans do. Therefore, granting any animal rights would be absurd.

One major flaw with this argument, says Peter Singer, father of the
animal liberation movement, is that humans who cannot make moral decisions are granted legal rights. The severely mentally disabled and the
unborn fetus, for example, enjoy protection under the law, even if they
are unable to understand or make ethical choices. Singer asserts, "On any
fair comparison of morally relevant characteristics, like rationality, self-
consciousness, awareness, autonomy, pleasure, pain, and so on, the calf,
the pig, and the much-derided chicken come out well ahead of the fetus
at any stage of pregnancy." Singer believes that any of those animals deserve more rights than an unborn child.

As can be clearly seen when examining the arguments of animal rights
advocates and opponents, determining whether and which animals should
be granted rights is exceedingly complex. The authors in *At Issue: Do Animals Have Rights?* debate many of the issues surrounding this question, such
as whether animal experimentation and cloning violate animals' rights.

1

Do Animals Have Rights?: The Debate

Roger Scruton and Andrew Tyler

Roger Scruton is a writer and philosopher who has published over thirty books, including Animal Rights and Wrongs *and* On Hunting. *Andrew Tyler, a former journalist, is the director of Animal Aid, the United Kingdom's largest animal rights group.*

Some people vehemently argue that humans violate animals' rights when they use animals for any purpose. Exploiting or killing farm and laboratory animals, they say, is just as immoral as enslaving or murdering humans. Others claim that although humans have duties to protect animals, they need not be restricted in their treatment of animals by the notion of rights, because animals cannot have rights and do not understand the duties that are tied to having rights. Furthermore, they say that the notion goes too far in granting all animals rights, including bugs and rodents. Such a concept is absurd, because humans are responsible for managing rampant animal populations, eliminating the carriers of disease, and restoring ecological balance, all of which are undermined by the idea of animal rights. Animal rights advocates retort that human intervention further disrupts the environment and is meant only to benefit humans, not animals.

Editor's Note: This is a series of letters between Roger Scruton and Andrew Tyler, later published in the Ecologist.

Dear Andrew Tyler
Many people now take the view that the human species is not entitled to the dominion that it has so far asserted over all other species. They express this by saying that animals, like us, have rights. Hence many of the things that we do to animals are morally indefensible. I find myself agreeing with the conclusion, but not with the premise. The attribution of rights to animals seems to me to be a radical departure from the norms of moral argument; if taken seriously it would undermine our abil-

ity to make the important decisions that we now must make if animals in general, and wild animals in particular, are to enjoy a sustainable future.

The debate is not a trivial one. Advocates of animal rights are currently attempting to bankrupt a firm (Huntingdon Life Sciences) which uses animals for medical research; they have succeeded in banning fur farming in Britain, and are now hopeful that they can ban hunting with hounds. They intend, if successful, to ban shooting and angling, and no doubt there are those among them who would like to impose a strict regime of non-interference in the entire animal kingdom, whether the rest of us want it or not.

This intransigence is an inevitable result of the belief in rights. If I believe that you are denying someone his rights—to life, limb, property or freedom—then I am absolutely entitled to interfere on the victim's behalf. Rights may be relinquished—but only by the person who possesses them, and only if his action is entirely voluntary. The purpose of the concept of a right is to establish, around each individual, a sphere where that individual alone is sovereign. Hence your right is my duty, and if I disregard your rights I both wrong you and also do what is wrong.

The attribution of rights to animals seems to me to be a radical departure from the norms of moral argument.

Why should we have such a concept? Surely, because we wish to live in a condition of mutual freedom and mutual respect. The concept of a right derives from legal ways of thinking, and serves as the individual's shield against oppression. All calculation stops at the threshold where you are sovereign, and it is to mark out this threshold that we deploy the concept of a right. Some philosophers believe that there are both positive rights—which are laid down by a legal code—and natural rights—which are inherent in our condition as rational agents. And it is this idea of a natural right that is invoked by those who argue for the rights of animals. Natural rights are those like the rights to life, limb and freedom, the violation of which is tantamount to a declaration of war.

Let us suppose that animals do have rights; what follows? Surely, the very least that follows is that it is wrong to kill them, to eat them, to keep them as pets, to make them suffer in any way that is not to their individual benefit—and wrong in just the way that it is wrong to do any of this to a human being. That is what the activists say they believe. But do they really believe it? Are they prepared to say that my attempts to rid my barn of rats are tantamount to mass murder? That people who keep cats are complicitous in serial killing? That my keeping a horse in his stable is a case of false imprisonment? That my digging the garden involves the negligent slaughter of innocent worms, beetles and moles? Which activities involving animals would be permitted, and on what grounds?

But there is a more important consequence of rights-talk from the environmental point of view. To invoke rights is to accord absolute respect to the individual, and to give him precedence over collective calculations whenever his vital interests are at stake. Hence the sick, the deformed, and the genetically impaired have just the same rights as the healthy and the strong. If animals have rights you have no more right to kill a sick, wounded or genetically impaired [creature] than you have to kill its healthy companion. All attempts at managing wildlife populations by encouraging healthy breeding and eliminating the carriers of diseases would be ruled out on moral grounds. It would also be morally impossible to intervene in nature to re-establish the ecological balance—say by culling an over-abundant predator population, by controlling parasites and pests, or by capturing animals and moving them to favourable breeding grounds.

Of course, if we lived in virgin forests as hunter-gatherers (itself morally impossible for the animal rights activist), we could reasonably assume that the ecological balance would restore itself over our footsteps. But we do not live like that. The environment is now our concern, something to be managed and restored by human ingenuity, and no longer able to restore itself unaided. To believe in the rights of animals we should have to relinquish that task, and allow animal populations to find what niche they can in the human sprawl. Good for rats and crows perhaps; but not for apes or fish or songbirds.

Roger Scruton

Dear Roger Scruton

You betray some panic over the inroads made by animal advocates. You complain that taking seriously the concept of animal rights represents a radical departure from 'the norms of moral argument', as though those often sterile, centuries-old 'norms' adequately serve us now . . . or ever did. Your notion of the absolute sovereignty of the human individual is a picture book romance, a conceit that has as much substance as candyfloss. More on this later.

> *Just as commercial, cultural and intellectual life thrived in Britain after we gave up trading in Africans, so [too is] there a positive future without exploiting animals.*

You're panicked about the campaign successes relating to Huntingdon Life Sciences (a morally, scientifically and near-financially bankrupt company); about the fur farming ban; and about further ambitions in the direction of bloodsports. These successes do not arise because animal rights people have doped the nation's drinking water but out of a rational objection to pointless animal abuse and a rejection of the flimsy justifications offered by those who orchestrate those abuses. The successes have come, notwithstanding a national media that, in the main, ardently promotes the status quo and which characterises effective dissent as mad and dangerous.

In such a climate, animal rights campaigners cannot possibly impose anything on the majority. Yet recent opinion polls show that most people oppose bloodsports, that vegetarianism is increasingly popular and that even opinion about animal experiments is finely balanced, despite ceaseless promotion of vivisection by the powerful scientific establishment, backed by government.

These poll showings indicate incipient, rather than grounded, support for the rights argument. It is the ambition of people like myself to encourage people into thinking further and acting accordingly—for example, into foregoing the enfeebled products of intensive animal farming and voicing opposition to vivisection—a practice that is a scientific nonsense, as well as an abuse of power, given that research data obtained from animals cannot be reliably applied to human beings.

We live in a world that we control. To relinquish that control is merely to opt out of our principal responsibility. And it will not benefit the animals.

I referred earlier to your invocation of the absolute sovereignty of the human individual. You say that this 'sovereignty' can be relinquished only voluntarily by the holder and that we are collectively bound (as individuals) to defend each other's rights. Where in the world, ever, has this seminar-room notion ever been played out? Western armed forces bombed Baghdad [Iraq, in 1998], killing many innocents because Saddam [Hussein's] regime wouldn't accede to inspections of its weapons facilities. I publicly objected. Did you? The street children of Rio [de Janeiro, Brazil] are shot dead, with government complicity, because they interfere with the tourist trade. A multinational pharmaceutical company arranged for a number of children to stand in a field in Egypt and be sprayed with an experimental pesticide so that it could collect toxicity data.

These are not unrepeatable travesties. This is the way of the world. The status quo is corrupt. The mighty trample the weak. Greed is rewarded. Decent sentiments are ever present but they are not sufficiently nurtured and celebrated by those at the commanding heights.

Yes, the notion of rights for human beings does exist thanks to centuries of struggle by oppressed groups. But while they are sacrosanct in the minds of some philosophers and in worthy pan-national Declarations, they truly exist only for so long as, and to the extent that, the subject groups can defend them.

Though they are deserving of them, non-human animals have precious few rights, even in theory. In law they are property. There are certain rules about how we may exploit, kill and consume animals. But protection for animals stops at the point where we, as the exploiting species, are seriously inconvenienced or deprived of profit or pleasure.

The modern animal rights movement is concerned to address this situation and demonstrate that, just as commercial, cultural and intellectual life thrived in Britain after we gave up trading in Africans, so there is a positive future without exploiting animals.

You must appreciate that ours is a practical movement. Our heads are not up our fundaments. We seek, first of all, to demonstrate what is often denied: that hundreds of millions of animals every year in Britain alone are unwarranted victims of human commerce and culture—and that this occurs because animals have the status of mere objects. We promote ways of living that eschew the flesh, secretions and skins of animals. We repudiate the trade in 'pets' (give a home to a sanctuary animal instead!) and oppose leisure pursuits that depend on harrying and/or demeaning other species. While it is impossible in this imperfect world to live an immaculate life, the first principle should be: do as little harm as possible.

Let me now deal with this nonsense about 'human ingenuity' being needed to ensure a sustainable future.

The case I've set out rests on a simple guiding principle, which I've already enunciated: do as little harm as possible.

This has come to mean scapegoating a range of 'alien' or commercially inexpedient species (from grey squirrels to badgers) for our own reckless excesses. The record shows that we fail when we try to poison and shoot our way to environmental harmony.

The record also shows that the only rational approach to take is to curb our own destructive appetites and to concede actual territory to non-human animals—not least to those from whom we are able to extract no obvious, or immediate advantage.

Andrew Tyler

Dear Andrew

The notion of a right, I suggested, is an expression of the sovereignty that human beings claim over their own lives, and is only doubtfully applied to creatures who do not understand moral ideas, and who have no conception of their duties. You dismiss this as a 'seminar-room notion', without, however, proposing any alternative definition. The only intellectual enlightenment that I can glean from your response is that animals have rights because you say so. But you don't tell me which rights, which animals, or what this permits or forbids us to do to them. I would ask you again whether the killing of a rat is murder? If not, why not?

You seem keen to attribute 'panic' to me, which makes it sound as though you were offering not arguments but threats. I am far from disputing the claim that people abuse animals, but if this is to give grounds for condemnation we need to be much clearer than you are prepared to be about the nature of moral judgement. You ridicule my reference to the norms of moral argument, but your reply would be a mere tissue of self-serving emotion if it did not have a moral base. By attributing rights to animals you are making a moral judgement: but I contend that you are making it in the wrong terms, and that the consequences of doing so are intellectual and moral confusion.

You say that it is 'nonsense' to suggest that human ingenuity is needed to ensure a sustainable future. But, however badly we have managed things up to now, there is still no doubt in my mind that the answer is not no management at all but better management. I believe that the animals on our farm are in a more sustainable equilibrium since we shot the magpies and crows that were eating the young of other birds, that the cows are more healthy since we got rid of the rats (not by poisoning, hasten to add), that the voles and the carp have a better deal since the mink-hounds came. You may disapprove of these forms of management, but without them there would be very little bio-diversity here above the level of insect-life, and that too needs management. Even in your Vegan utopia, crops would have to be protected from pests, and bio-diversity maintained by intervention.

Of course, if animals have rights then everything I have just described is morally wrong—indeed, morally impossible. You may think that, but since you have given no argument for it, and since I believe that the consequences of laissez faire [uninvolvement] would now be bad not only for us but for animals too, I reject your conclusion. It is good to feel sympathy for animals, to protect them and to do what you can to provide for their needs. But this does not alter the fact that it is we who do these things, because we live in a world that we control. To relinquish that control is merely to opt out of our principal responsibility. And it will not benefit the animals, even if it makes us feel good about them.

What you are really describing is the duties of humans, not the rights of animals.

Of course animals are not 'mere objects'. They are sentient beings, towards whom we have real obligations. I sympathise with your aversion to the trade in pets, partly because I think it encourages people to see animals as persons, and so to degrade both themselves and their pets. And like you I would like to see more territory conceded to the animals. But this conceding of territory would be a form of management too, with people making all the important choices, and interfering to maintain things when pests, diseases or forest fires become a threat.

Roger Scruton

Dear Roger

How odd! I set out an unequivocal case for non-violence against people and animals and you suggest I'm offering you 'threats'. . . .

The panic I detected seemed to be rooted in your unease at the way the world is changing beneath your feet. The old conceits are fast unravelling—eg that killing animals for pleasure, money, or out of expediency is somehow a noble project.

The rights I would accord non-human animals are the rights not to be killed by humans—except unwittingly or in self-defence. Also, freedom from torture and exploitation. Those rights would extend to all species, which on the balance of the evidence, are sentient. I'm not concerned to judge and police other species in regard to their dealings with each other. Those who attempt such things have shown they have neither the requisite competence nor the vision. Besides, while some animals might kill others, they don't have our species' capacity for grandly choreographed, industrialised destruction.

Is killing a rat murder? Rats usually proliferate because people provide unguarded food sources. I know many animal rights people who farm, run factories and other businesses and are able to discourage unwelcome animals by non-violent means. Killing is lazy and nearly always futile: the vacuum left by the slain animal is filled by another, unless preventive measures are taken. So yes, killing a rat is unwarranted and immoral. But apply the term murder and, because of cultural conditioning, people react rather than think. So I wouldn't use it. But consider this: if someone encourages another to kill my child, most people would see that as aiding and abetting a murder. But what if a person publicly endorses a policy of aerial bombing that kills children (all of them sovereign, according to your formulation) thousands of miles away. Is that also aiding and abetting? My answer is yes, but distance and cultural bubblewrap get in the way.

Your concern is that the extension of rights to animals would mean a curtailment of the freedom that people of your disposition currently enjoy to exploit and kill.

The case I've set out rests on a simple guiding principle, which I've already enunciated: do as little harm as possible. That is the test I would always apply, whilst appreciating that none of us can tread the earth without doing some damage.

The case you've set out against animal rights, it seems to me, rests on a pernicious conceit. It is that the world's flora and fauna benefits from human beings' 'stewardship'. The stewardship you favour involves identifying various problem species and slaughtering them; and identifying other species as having utility (cattle, sheep, cows, chickens, pheasants) and producing them in vast numbers, then killing them for food or sport.

The world resulting from such stewardship is polluted, over-heated, and unequal. It is locked into an unsustainable food production system that produces diseased animals and has seen the death of forests, the uprooting of thousands of miles of hedgerow, the prolific use of toxic chemicals and the imperilling of numerous species of songbird, mammal and fish, as well as a host of wildflowers and other plant life.

One of your favourite themes is that animals are not part of a 'moral community'. They are undeserving of rights because they have no duties or responsibilities. Clearly, you have much to learn about the richness of animal culture—of animals' powerful social bonds, their capacity for grief and sensual pleasure, their ability to think strategically and work cooperatively. The magpie feels no duty towards you, but then why should he? You want him dead.

Andrew Tyler

Dear Andrew

Rights protect the individual, not the species. By attributing rights to animals, therefore, we tie our hands when it comes to the great environmental questions that now confront us. You think that our hands ought to be tied: since animals have rights, then all culling, even of the diseased and the dangerous, is morally impossible.

You believe that animals have the 'right not to be killed by humans', but you do not judge and police other species. Presumably therefore you don't believe that a mouse has a 'right not to be killed by a cat'. I take this to show that all this talk of rights is so much hot air. What you are really describing is the duties of humans, not the rights of animals.

You refer to the 'richness of animal culture', and (in certain cases) this is an apt description—even of the rats in our ditches (which do not proliferate because we leave unguarded food, as you would like to believe). But that does not imply that animals organise their lives by moral principles, or that they blame and condemn each other as we do (and as you do preeminently), or that they settle their disputes by judgement and law. It is because we respond to the call of duty that we can be, and ought to be, stewards of our environment, and not just one competing species among many.

The world is polluted and over-heated not because of stewardship but because of bad stewardship. If everybody thought as you do, this would, I believe, simply entrench the position of humanity as the dominant species, while leaving all others to fend for themselves in a constantly dwindling habitat. It is fair enough to live by the principle 'Do as little harm as possible', in a world that is in a state of ecological balance. But that is not our world. I would prefer to say, when it comes to questions of the environment, 'Do as much good as possible'. That may mean also doing harm, and not only to rats.

Roger Scruton

Dear Roger

You equate culling with 'stewardship' and still fail to acknowledge the mess we've made in this area. You suggest, instead, that all will be remedied by a bit of sensible tweaking.

Fewer mice—and birds—would be killed by cats if cats weren't mass produced for the pet industry. I don't believe, in any case, that you are remotely concerned about crimes against mice by cats. Your concern is that the extension of rights to animals would mean a curtailment of the freedom that people of your disposition currently enjoy to exploit and kill.

I clipped a book review you wrote for *The Times* in December 1996. The volume, by a 'pious Catholic' and public school Classics master, described the author's 'sporting' exploits in Cumbria [Great Britain]. You wrote approvingly of his 'defiant celebration of the act of killing fish and birds in quantities that far surpass his gastronomic capacity . . . I find nothing strange' you declared, 'in the fact that these activities should be the high point of someone's life, and the object of powerful religious feelings.'

You tell me that your objective is to 'do as much good as possible'. Is this an example?

The movement for animal rights is another chapter in the history of social progress movements that has included the abolition of human slavery and the enfranchisement of women and the 'lower orders'. That Animal Aid recognises the continuity of such struggles is evidenced by the Living Without Cruelty Exhibition we staged in March 2000. [International rights groups] Oxfam, Amnesty, World Development Movement, and Fairtrade Foundation were among the participants.

The animal rights movement is inclusive of anyone whose goal is a new, fairer deal for animals. Our view is that it is better to go part of the way towards a cruelty-free lifestyle than obstruct the way forward with blinkered and inconsistent hostility.

Andrew Tyler

2
Animals Have Rights

Tom Regan

A leader in the contemporary animal rights movement, philosopher Tom Regan has written several books on animal rights and is university alumni distinguished professor at North Carolina State University.

It is irrational to discriminate against animals. People who believe humans are superior to animals are practicing speciesism, a prejudice much like sexism or racism. The philosophy that animals have the same rights as humans, on the other hand, is unprejudiced, unselfish, and just. Treating animals with respect fosters individual growth and helps society become more compassionate. The idea of animal rights is also peace loving; it advocates that humans should end the war against animals.

It is not rational to discriminate arbitrarily. And discrimination against nonhuman animals is arbitrary. It is wrong to treat weaker human beings, especially those who are lacking in normal human intelligence, as "tools" or "renewable resources" or "models" or "commodities." It cannot be right, therefore, to treat other animals as if they were "tools," "models" and the like, if their psychology is as rich as (or richer than) these humans. To think otherwise is irrational.

The philosophy of animal rights is respectful of our best science in general and evolutionary biology in particular. The latter teaches that, in Charles Darwin's words, humans differ from many other animals "in degree, not in kind." Questions of line drawing to one side, it is obvious that the animals used in laboratories, raised for food, and hunted for pleasure or trapped for profit, for example, are our psychological kin. This is not fantasy, this is fact, proven by our best science.

The philosophy of animal rights is unprejudiced

Racists are people who think that the members of their race are superior to the members of other races simply because the former belong to their (the "superior") race. Sexists believe that the members of their sex are superior to the members of the opposite sex simply because the former belong to their (the "superior") sex. Both racism and sexism are paradigms of unsupportable bigotry. There is no "superior" or "inferior" sex or race. Racial and sexual differences are biological, not moral, differences.

The same is true of speciesism—the view that members of the species *Homo sapiens* are superior to members of every other species simply because human beings belong to one's own (the "superior") species. For there is no "superior" species. To think otherwise is to be no less prejudiced than racists or sexists.

The philosophy of animal rights is just

Justice is the highest principle of ethics. We are not to commit or permit injustice so that good may come, not to violate the rights of the few so that the many might benefit. Slavery allowed this. Child labor allowed this. Most examples of social injustice allow this. But not the philosophy of animal rights, whose highest principle is that of justice: No one has a right to benefit as a result of violating another's rights, whether that "other" is a human being or some other animal.

A full human life demands feelings of empathy and sympathy—in a word, compassion—for the victims of injustice, whether the victims are humans or other animals. The philosophy of animal rights calls for, and its acceptance fosters the growth of, the virtue of compassion. This philosophy is, in Lincoln's words, "the way of a whole human being."

There is no "superior" species. To think otherwise is to be no less prejudiced than racists or sexists.

The philosophy of animal rights demands a commitment to serve those who are weak and vulnerable—those who, whether they are humans or other animals, lack the ability to speak for or defend themselves, and who are in need of protection against human greed and callousness. This philosophy requires this commitment, not because it is in our self-interest to give it, but because it is right to do so. This philosophy therefore calls for, and its acceptance fosters the growth of, unselfish service.

The philosophy of animal rights is progressive

All the great traditions in ethics, both secular and religious, emphasize the importance of four things: knowledge, justice, compassion, and autonomy. The philosophy of animal rights is no exception. This philosophy teaches that our choices should be based on knowledge, should be expressive of compassion and justice, and should be freely made. It is not easy to achieve these virtues, or to control the human inclinations toward greed and indifference. But a whole human life is impossible without them. The philosophy of animal rights both calls for, and its acceptance fosters the growth of, individual self-fulfillment.

The greatest impediment to the flourishing of human society is the exploitation of other animals at human hands. This is true in the case of unhealthy diets, of the habitual reliance on the "whole animal model" in science, and of the many other forms animal exploitation takes. And it is no less true of education and advertising, for example, which help deaden the human psyche to the demands of reason, impartiality, compassion, and justice. In all these ways (and more), nations remain profoundly backward because they fail to serve the true interests of their citizens.

The philosophy of animal rights is environmentally wise

The major cause of environmental degradation, including the greenhouse effect, water pollution, and the loss both of arable land and top soil, for example, can be traced to the exploitation of animals. This same pattern exists throughout the broad range of environmental problems, from acid rain and ocean dumping of toxic wastes, to air pollution and the destruction of natural habitat. In all these cases, to act to protect the affected animals (who are, after all, the first to suffer and die from these environmental ills), is to act to protect the earth.

The philosophy of animal rights is peace loving

The fundamental demand of the philosophy of animal rights is to treat humans and other animals with respect. To do this requires that we not harm anyone just so that we ourselves or others might benefit. This philosophy therefore is totally opposed to military aggression. It is a philosophy of peace. But it is a philosophy that extends the demand for peace beyond the boundaries of our species. For there is a war being waged, every day, against countless millions of nonhuman animals. To stand truly for peace is to stand firmly against speciesism. It is wishful thinking to believe that there can be "peace in the world" if we fail to bring peace to our dealings with other animals.

3

Great Apes Should Be Granted Legal Rights

Great Ape Project

The Great Ape Project advocates that since great apes possess characteristics and emotions that people consider morally important, they should be considered as persons and granted the same basic legal rights as people enjoy.

Due to their humanlike mental capacities and emotions, great apes deserve the rights to life, liberty, and the prohibition of torture, including that which is imposed on them by scientific research. Because great apes are unable to defend themselves against humans, the law must protect their rights and allow them to live free from unnecessary human intervention. They can be denied these rights only if they are clearly a danger to others.

The Great Ape Project is an idea, a book, and an organization.

The idea is radical but simple: to include the non-human great apes within the community of equals by granting them the basic moral and legal protection that only human beings currently enjoy.

The book, which is the collective work of a group of scientists and scholars, is a multi-faceted argument against the unthinking denial of fundamental rights to beings who are not members of our own species, but who quite evidently possess many of the characteristics that we consider morally important.

The organization is an international group founded to work for the removal of the non-human great apes from the category of property, and for their immediate inclusion within the category of *persons*.

The Declaration on Great Apes

We demand the extension of the community of equals to include all great apes: human beings, chimpanzees, bonobos, gorillas and orang-utans. The "community of equals" is the moral community within which we accept certain basic moral principles or rights as governing our relations with each other and enforceable at law. Among these principles or rights are the following:

1. *The Right to Life*

The lives of members of the community of equals are to be protected. Members of the community of equals may not be killed except in very strictly defined circumstances, for example, self-defence.

2. *The Protection of Individual Liberty*

Members of the community of equals are not to be arbitrarily deprived of their liberty; if they should be imprisoned without due legal process, they have the right to immediate release. The detention of those who have not been convicted of any crime, or of those who are not criminally liable, should be allowed only where it can be shown to be for their own good, or necessary to protect the public from a member of the community who would clearly be a danger to others if at liberty. In such cases, members of the community of equals must have the right to appeal, either directly or, if they lack the relevant capacity, through an advocate, to a judicial tribunal.

3. *The Prohibition of Torture*

The deliberate infliction of severe pain on a member of the community of equals, either wantonly or for an alleged benefit to others, is regarded as torture, and is wrong.

Goals

Anyone who indicates their endorsement of the Declaration on Great Apes can become a supporter of the organization, which takes the Anti-Slavery Society as its political model. We already have supporters in more than twenty nations. We will start operating at a national level in as many countries as possible. Activities range from public education, to campaigning, to the adoption of individual imprisoned non-human great apes. From small-scale, local interventions, we will work up towards an international level, so as to bring about a momentous but well-grounded change in the status of chimpanzees, gorillas and orang-utans.

Our long-term goal is a United Nations Declaration of the Rights of Great Apes. When this historic result has been achieved, we will advocate the setting up of guarded territories so that chimpanzees, gorillas, bonobos and orang-utans can continue to live as free beings in their own ways.

Extending the community of equals

The following text is taken from the book *The Great Ape Project: Equality Beyond Humanity.*

> "At present, only members of the species *homo sapiens* are regarded as members of the community of equals. The inclusion, for the first time, of non-human animals into this community is an ambitious project. The chimpanzee (including in this term both *pan troglodytes* and the pygmy chimpanzee, *pan paniscus*), the gorilla, *gorilla gorilla*, and the orang-utan, *pongo pygmaeus*, are the closest relatives of our species. They also have mental capacities and an emotional

life sufficient to justify inclusion within the community of equals. To the objection that chimpanzees, gorillas and orang-utans will be unable to defend their own claims within the community, we respond that human guardians should safeguard their interests and rights, in the same ways as the interests of young or intellectually disabled members of our own species are safeguarded."

Our request comes at a special moment in history. Never before has our dominion over other animals been so pervasive and systematic. Yet this is also the moment when, within that very Western civilization that has so inexorably extended this dominion, a rational ethic has emerged challenging the moral significance of membership of our own species. This challenge seeks equal consideration for the interests of all animals, human and non-human.

"Human guardians should safeguard [the] interests and rights [of great apes], in the same ways as the interests of young or intellectually disabled members of our own species are safeguarded."

It has given rise to a political movement, still fluid but growing. The slow but steady widening of the scope of the golden rule "treat others as you would have them treat you" has now resumed its course. The notion of 'us' as opposed to 'the other', which, like a more and more abstract silhouette, assumed in the course of centuries the contours of the boundaries of the tribe, of the nation, of the race, of the human species, and which for a time the species barrier had congealed and stiffened has again become something alive, ready for further change.

The Great Ape Project aims at taking just one step in this process of extending the community of equals. We shall provide ethical argument, based on scientific evidence about the capacities of gorillas, chimpanzees, bonobos and orang-utans, for taking this step. Whether this step should also be the first of many others is not for the Great Ape Project to say. No doubt some of us, speaking individually, would want to extend the community of equals to many other animals as well; others may consider that extending the community to include all great apes is as far as we should go at present. We leave the consideration of that question for another occasion.

Responding to criticisms

We have not forgotten that we live in a world in which, for at least three-quarters of the human population, the idea of human rights is no more than rhetoric, and not a reality in everyday life. In such a world, the idea of equality for non-human animals, even for those disquieting doubles of ours, the other great apes, may not be received with much favour. We recognize, and deplore, the fact that all over the world human beings are living without basic rights or even the means for a decent subsistence. The denial of the basic rights of particular other species will not, however, assist the world's poor and oppressed to win their just struggles. Nor is it reasonable to ask that the members of these other species should wait until all humans have achieved their rights first. That suggestion itself assumes that beings belonging to other species are of lesser moral significance than human beings. Moreover, on present indications, the suggested delay might well be an extremely long one.

Another basis for opposition to our demand may arise from the fact that the great apes—especially chimpanzees—are considered to be extremely valuable laboratory tools. Of course, since the main object of research is to learn about human beings, the ideal subject of study would be the human being. Harmful research on non-consenting human beings is, however, rightly regarded as unethical. Because harmful research on non-consenting chimpanzees, orang-utans, gorillas or bonobos is not seen in the same light, researchers are permitted to do things to these great apes that would be considered utterly abhorrent if done to human beings. Indeed, the value of the other great apes as research tools lies precisely in the combination of two conflicting factors: on the one hand, the fact that, both physically and psychologically, they very closely resemble our own species; and on the other, the fact that they are denied the ethical and legal protection that we give to our own species.

Success is possible

Those who wish to defend the present routine treatment of the non-human great apes in laboratories and in other circumstances—disturbing detail of which we present in [*The Great Ape Project: Equality Beyond Humanity*]—must now bear the burden of proof in refuting the case we make . . . for including all great apes within the community of equals. If our arguments cannot be refuted, the way in which great apes other than humans are now treated will be shown to be an arbitrary and unjustifiable form of discrimination. For this, there will no longer be any excuse.

The resolution of a moral dispute is often just the beginning, not the end, of a social question. We know that, even if we can prove our view to be sound, we will still be far away from the moment when the dispersed members of the chimpanzee, gorilla, bonobo and orang-utan species can be liberated and lead their different lives as equals in their own special territories in our countries, or free in the equatorial forests to which they once belonged. As normally happens when ethical progress runs its course, the obstacles will be many, and opposition from those whose interests are threatened will be strong. . . .

Unlike some oppressed groups that have achieved equality, chimpanzees, gorillas, bonobos and orang-utans are unable to fight for themselves. Will we find the social forces prepared to fight on their behalf to bring about their inclusion within the community of equals? We believe that success is possible. While some oppressed humans have achieved victory through their own struggles, others have been as powerless as chimpanzees, gorillas and orang-utans are today. History shows us that there has always been, within our own species, that saving factor: a squad of determined people willing to overcome the selfishness of their own group in order to advance another's cause.

4

Animals Should Not Be Granted Legal Rights

David R. Carlin

David R. Carlin is professor of philosophy and sociology at the Community College of Rhode Island.

By arguing that animals are equal to humans and thus deserve the same legal protection, animal rights proponents reduce human beings to nothing more than biological entities, on par with animals. Animal rights advocates' view of humanity negates fundamental Christian, Platonic, and Stoic claims that man was created in the image and likeness of God. Humans are clearly superior to animals. Granting animals legal rights would be dangerous and degrading to humans.

[In 1999] Harvard Law School offered its first-ever course on animal rights. This is good news for animal rights advocates, since Harvard is one of the two or three top law schools in the nation. If Harvard is on board for animal rights, can the Supreme Court be far behind?

Currently, American law gives animals *protection* in a wide variety of circumstances, but it affords them no *rights*. The prevailing legal principle is that only persons can be bearers of fights. So, before animals can have rights, either that principle will have to be changed, or it will have to be shown that animals (at least some of them) are persons.

The animal rights movement degrades humans

The animal rights movement (of which Peter Singer, the controversial Princeton professor, is the philosophical guru) contends that there should be only a relatively narrow legal gap between humans and animals. Biologically speaking, of course, there *is* only a narrow gap between humans and the highest of the animals. But this raises the question: Is a strictly biological account of human nature adequate? The animal rights movement would answer this question in the affirmative; Christianity, by contrast, has always answered it in the negative. At first glance, the animal rights movement seems to be aiming at the elevation of animals. In fact, however, it is but the latest episode in a long history of attempts to degrade humans.

Many individual members of the animal rights movement, I willingly concede, are kindhearted folks who are revolted at cruelty to animals and wish to minimize it; they have no desire to degrade humanity. But historical movements often have objective tendencies that contradict the wishes of their proponents. (Witness communism, which, despite its objective tendency to tyranny and mass murder, had many followers who were humane and philanthropic in intention.) Underlying the push for narrowing the legal gap between humans and animals is the philosophical premise that there is no more than a narrow ontological gap between humans and animals. But the animal rights people are not the first to embrace this premise. Far from it.

Like humans, animals are rational

In the sixteenth century, Michel de Montaigne, the great French essayist and skeptic, argued that the gap between humans and animals was narrower than most people imagined. He devoted much of his writing to showing that humans are not nearly as rational as we, in our pride, suppose ourselves to be, while occasionally pointing out how surprisingly rational the lower animals could sometimes be. In his most comprehensive and influential essay, "An Apology for Raimond Sebond," Montaigne cited the case of a logical dog, a case reported by an ancient philosopher. The dog was following a scent along a path. Suddenly the single path divided into three. The dog hesitated: Which way to go? He sniffed at one path; no scent. He sniffed at a second; no scent there either. And then, without bothering to give an investigatory sniff at the one remaining, he set off on this third path. Clearly the dog had performed a disjunctive syllogism, saying to himself: "The scent I'm following will be found either on path A, B, or C; it is not found on A or B; it follows, therefore, that it must be on C."

And since, according to the dominant philosophical tradition of Montaigne's day—a tradition that reached back to Plato, Aristotle, and the Stoics—rationality (or a capacity for logical thinking) is the distinctive characteristic of human beings, it was no small thing to show that dogs as well as humans can be logical. In the world of philosophy, it had always been rationality that established the almost infinite ontological gap between humans and animals. Show that rationality is a characteristic shared by both, and humanity's ancient claim to dominance is destroyed.

Communication and survival

Near the middle of the eighteenth century, during the robust early stages of the Enlightenment, a minor French philosophe, Julien Offray de la Mettrie, wrote a book titled *L'Homme Machine*. If humans are nothing more than machines, he argued, albeit very refined and complex ones, then there is certainly no great ontological gap between humans and the lower animals, for they are also machines, though less refined and complex. La Mettrie suggested, for instance, that the reason apes cannot speak is not because of any inferiority in rationality to human beings but because of "some defect in the organs of speech." He believed a young ape could be taught the use of language if we were to instruct it using the (then newly invented) methods used to teach deaf-mutes to "speak." In other words, given the right teacher, apes could be taught sign language.

The animal rights movement seems to be aiming at the elevation of animals. . . . However, it . . . attempts to degrade humans.

But to date, the greatest of all attempts to narrow the gap between humans and the lower animals has been Darwinism. Perhaps this should not be said of the Darwinism of Darwin himself, who had little wish, at least in public, to extrapolate his biological findings into the realm of ontology. But it can certainly be said of many of Darwin's epigones, who viewed humans as purely biological entities and thus regarded biology as competent to pronounce the last word on the ontological rank of human nature. Since humans have the same remote ancestry as the rest of the animal kingdom, since we have the same relatively proximate ancestry as the great apes, and since anatomically we bear a strong resemblance to these our "cousins," then it follows (they reasoned) that humans are ontologically only a little bit superior to the lower animals. And if we measure superiority and inferiority in terms of capacity to survive (which is perhaps the true Darwinian way of measuring these things), then we are not superior at all; for it is obvious that all surviving animal species have equally met that test. By that measure, our superiority, if we are indeed superior, will not be shown until we outlast all other animal species; but that is almost certainly impossible, since it is difficult to imagine how humans could survive on earth without the assistance of other simultaneously existing animal species.

Why narrow the gap?

Our contemporary animal rights movement is heir to this long tradition of trying to narrow the gap between humans and lower animals. But what motive lies behind this tradition? The answer seems obvious enough. Specifically, the motive is anti-Christian; more generally, it is a strong animosity toward the view of human nature taken both by biblical religions and by the great classical schools of philosophy, especially Platonism and Stoicism. That man is "made in the image and likeness of God" is an expression found in the Bible, but it is a formula that well expresses the anthropology of Plato and the Stoics as well. To reduce human nature to nothing more than its biological status is to attack this ancient and exalted conception of human nature.

In defense of the attackers—from Montaigne, through the philosophes and the Darwinians, to Peter Singer (who once wrote a book titled *Animal Liberation*) and the Harvard Law School—it might be said that their intentions have often been humane. The Stoic-Christian theory of human nature, in their opinion, has been dangerously unrealistic, the product not of empirical observation but of fantastic imagination. By encouraging men and women to believe that their true home is not in this world, the world of nature—that we are potentially divine beings living in temporary exile—this fantastic theory has rendered humans unable to achieve such limited happiness we might have achieved. Demoting human nature from heaven to earth will, by making us more realistic, render us more successful. Better (in [Lord Thomas Babington] Macaulay's phrase) to own an acre in Middlesex than a county in Utopia.

Animals should not be granted rights

This defense ("they had good intentions") might have been acceptable prior to the twentieth century. But in the course of that century we had some unpleasant experiences with persons who entertained the purely biological conception of human nature. [Adolf] Hitler was a great believer in this purely biological conception (sometimes with a confused overlay of pagan romanticism). In his way, he can be counted as one of Darwin's epigones. Now, of course, you cannot prove that an idea is wrong simply because Hitler embraced it; for instance, that Hitler favored the production of Volkswagens doesn't prove that they are bad automobiles. But when there is a direct link between one of his major ideas and the Holocaust, as there is in the case of his conception of human nature, this is at least enough to give us pause. At present I cannot *prove* that the idea of animal rights is extraordinarily dangerous and inhumane; to get proof of this, we'll have to wait until the disastrous consequences of the idea reveal themselves over the next century or so. But I strongly suspect that it's a dangerous idea, and accordingly I suspect that the promoters of this idea, whatever their intentions, are enemies of the human race.

5

Animal Experimentation Is Unethical

S.F. Sapontzis

S.F. Sapontzis, author of Moral, Reasons, and Animals, *served on the Institutional Animal Care and Use Committee of the Lawrence Berkeley Laboratory.*

Just as it is unethical to conduct research on humans who have not consented to it, it is wrong to experiment on animals. Humans may benefit from the results of research, but this does not justify injuring or killing other creatures any more than a father is justified in stealing food from another child to feed his own. Additionally, although animals may not be autonomous, they do have interests, which human guardians must be assigned to protect. Lastly, if humans are in fact superior to animals, then they have obligations to protect them from harm and exploitation.

Norman led Jennie into the laboratory and had her sit on a metal table near the windows. She sat quietly while Norman fitted her with a helmet containing electrial monitors and couplings for attaching the helmet to other devices. She was watching people walking across the lawn. When Norman finished, she had to lie down while the helmet was secured to a large machine and her arms and legs were secured to a table. All she could see now was the ceiling. Norman hooked up the monitoring devices in the helmet to a large console, checked out his equipment, then turned it on. Jennie's head was given a tremendous blow by a piston that crashed into her helmet. She was knocked unconscious and stayed that way while Norman pried off her helmet. When she regained consciousness, she went into convulsions for two minutes. When the convulsions stopped, Norman ran some tests on her. She was blind now and could not control her arms sufficiently to grasp and carry to her mouth some food placed in her hands. Finally, she was wheeled into another room where she was given an injection. Jennie died in less than a minute, and Norman began the work of decapitating her, describing the condition of her brain, and preparing slices of her brain tissue for microscopic analysis.

S.F. Sapontzis, "Unethical Considerations: Probing Animal Research," *AV Magazine*, Spring 2002, pp. 6–8. Copyright © 2002 by *AV Magazine*. Reproduced by permission.

Unethical research

This vignette is based on real research done on monkeys. Doing this research on humans would have been more efficient, since the goal was to develop therapies for human head injury victims, but running such tests on humans would be grossly unethical. Why is it not also unethical to run such tests on primates? That is the core ethical question concerning animal research: Why is it ethical to exploit animals in research when so exploiting humans would be ethically intolerable?

I will analyze the three strongest positive answers to that question, but first I want to emphasize that the most common justification for animal research is irrelevant to this question. That justification is that animal research benefits people. Many animal rights advocates doubt this, but even if all animal research resulted in human benefits, the question of whether the research was ethically justified would remain. That this is so can be quickly indicated by two comparisons. If research like that described above were done on humans, it would—like Nazi research on humans—be ethically deplored even if it benefited other people. Second, presumably, slavery benefited slave owners, but it is an ethically unacceptable institution, nonetheless. That one group benefits by exploiting another does not justify that exploitation. It follows that the fact that we may benefit by exploiting animals in research does not show that that exploitation is ethically justified.

Even if all animal research resulted in human benefits, the question of whether the research was ethically justified would remain.

But ethics requires justification for taking advantage of others. Here are relevant attempts to justify exploitative animal research.

The human community claim

Because we form a human community, we have special obligations to other people that we do not have to animals, since they cannot participate in this community. We are thereby obligated to protect and further human interests in ways we are not obligated to for animals interests, and this both justifies our sacrificing animal interests for human benefit and prohibits our exploiting humans in research.

Exploitation is not justified

Not only does ordinary ethics not require us to treat all animals equally, it does not require us to treat all people equally. However, a world in which we treated each other not as children, parents, siblings, friends, neighbors, colleagues, fellow citizens, etc., but merely as persons is not our ethical ideal. It would be a sadly impoverished place, devoid of many of the emotional relations that make life worth living.

Such reminders of the diversity of ethics discredit abstract theories of equality. Nonetheless, one of the primary functions of ethics, especially of basic rights, is to inhibit favoritism. While a father is ethically justified in giving priority to his child's interests, he would not be justified in doing so by taking food from another needy child, by enslaving a stranger, or by killing a business competitor. A father can be ethically criticized even for lavishing luxuries on his child while contributing nothing to help starving children in other parts of the world.

Even if we postulate humanistic obligations we have to all humans but to no animals, . . . it does not follow that we are justified in harming animals to fulfill those obligations.

Thus, in addition to special obligations to family, friends, etc., ordinary ethics contains egalitarian rights and responsibilities restricting the ways in which special obligations may be fulfilled. It follows that this human community defense of exploitative animal research cannot suffice. That we have obligations to one group which we do not have to another does not establish that we would be justified in exploiting that second group in order to fulfill our obligations to the first. For example, the special obligations we have to our friends would not justify our harming strangers to fulfill those obligations. Therefore, even if we postulate humanistic obligations we have to all humans but to no animals, such as an obligation to help people who are ill, it does not follow that we are justified in harming animals to fulfill those obligations. An argument showing that we are justified in fulfilling these special, humanistic obligations by exploiting those to whom we are not thus obligated must be provided before this defense of exploitative animal research can fulfill its purpose. Justifications [that follow] try to meet that need.

The informed consent argument

People would have to be coerced into participating in animal research, rather like the Nazi concentration camp experiments. It is such violations of the freedom and self-determination, what philosophers call 'autonomy' of rational beings, that makes actions unethical. However, free, informed consent cannot be an issue with animals, since they are not rational, autonomous beings. Consequently, as long as experiments are humane, there cannot be anything unethical about using animals in research.

Humans should protect animals' interests

There probably are as many people who believe that since animals cannot consent to being research subjects, animal research is ethically impermissible as there are people who believe that this inability removes humane animal research from ethical questioning. Both extremes are mistaken.

Young children cannot consent to participate in research, but this is neither an obstacle to doing any research with them nor a justification for humanely sacrificing their interests. Rather, the power to consent is given to someone who understands the interests of the children and is intent on protecting and furthering those interests.

Arguing by analogy, the conclusion to be drawn from animals' inability to consent is that guardians who understand the animals' interests and are intent on protecting and furthering those interests should be assigned to protect the animals. It would be the responsibility of such guardians to insure that research either was innocuous to the animals, was intended to be therapeutic for them, or provided them adequate compensation. Since a primary reason for doing laboratory research on animals is that the research procedure is detrimental to the interests of the research subjects, empowering animal guardians would drastically curtail laboratory animal research.

> *Our immediate experience of animals as feeling beings shows they have interests. The practice of performing pain and despair research on animals confirms this.*

Some philosophers contend that animals cannot have interests. I will not spend time answering such arguments because they are both technical and unconvincing and have been refuted elsewhere. Our immediate experience of animals as feeling beings shows they have interests. The practice of performing pain and despair research on animals confirms this. And that we are unsure whether worms and flies feel pain no more discredits our confidence that dogs do than it shows we cannot really know whether human infants like some things and dislike others.

The claim that humans are superior

Human life is ethically more worthy than animal life; consequently, we are justified in sacrificing these 'lower' life forms to protect and enhance human life. Sacrificing humans in research would, of course, not result in this exchange of lesser for greater worth and would, consequently, not be justified.

Flaws in the superiority argument

Ultimately, it is our belief that human life is worth more than animal life and that this justifies our sacrificing animals for our benefit. That explains why ordinary ethics does not protect animals against exploitation. However, both parts of this belief are unjustified.

Traditionally, our rationality is cited as what gives human life superior worth. Often, our ability to use reason to control our lives and surroundings is what is praised. This ability has even been called the image of God, the creator and controller of the universe, in us. However, citing our ability to dominate and control as justification for exploiting our 'inferiors' is to say that might makes right—not an ethical argument.

Some philosophers have argued that our superior worth derives from our being ethical agents, which requires normal human intelligence, since ethical agents must be able to recognize impersonal rules, control their appetites, and be motivated by a sense of duty. Such philosophers forget that generous sentiments are as ethically admirable as a sense of duty. Loving parents are, if anything, superior to merely dutiful parents. It follows that we are not the only ethical agents, since many animals, from loyal dogs to industrious beavers, are capable of unselfish action. Given our destructive, exploitative history, it is not obvious that we are the most ethical species, either.

Other philosophers contend that our reason makes us superior by enriching our lives, creating 'the good life' which is the goal of ethics. However, since none of us can actually experience the pleasures and fulfillments enjoyed by dolphins, dogs, or any other animal, we cannot really compare the quality of their lives to ours. This assertion of superiority is merely an expression of species bias.

Another argument is that our greater intelligence allows us to fight diseases, cultivate food, and otherwise enhance the quality of life. However, if we include our impact on the quality of life for animals other than ourselves, we produce less enjoyment and fulfillment than distress and frustration.

Thus, our firm belief in the superior worth of rational human life is probably just an expression of irrational instinct.

Inferiors should not be exploited

Let us presume what we just questioned, that human life is superior in an ethically significant way. Many people presume this justifies exploiting our 'inferiors,' but that is not so.

Ethically superior beings sometimes have extensive obligations to and only circumscribed privileges over their 'inferiors,' as in the case of human adults dealing with young children. Religion teaches that heavenly beings are far superior to us but not that this entitles them to exploit us. Indeed, those who do that thereby lose their superiority.

If our being impartial ethical agents or potential benefactors for life on earth is what makes us superior, it would be self-contradictory to claim that human superiority justifies out sacrificing the interests of 'inferiors' to fulfill our wants and needs. Just as the philosopher-kings of the ideal society designed by the philosopher Plato were prohibited from exploiting those whom their superior intellects obligated them to govern, so the correlate of our superior intellect is not the license to exploit animals but the obligation to care for them.

Current animal research practices are expressions of an aristocratic world view in which we humans are entitled to treat our 'inferiors' as resources for the preservation and enhancement of our supposedly superior way of life. Rejecting aristocratic world views is the touchstone of ethical progress. Our rejection of slavery, feudalism, and sexual and racial discrimination all involve discrediting supposed natural hierarchies in favor of a presumption of equal consideration for all. Therefore, eliminating aristocratic bias from animal research would contribute to continuing ethical progress.

6

Animal Experimentation Is Ethical

Henry E. Heffner

A psychology professor at the University of Toledo, Henry E. Heffner has conducted several experiments involving animals. He has published numerous articles, some of which concern the ethics of animal research.

Animals and humans depend on, and benefit from, each other. In this close relationship, anything that ensures the survival of humans, such as medical research, also furthers the well-being of animals. For this research, humans breed animals under controlled conditions, increasing both their numbers and genetic diversity. These animals live healthier, longer lives than they would in the wild.

In recent years the ethical basis for the use of animals by humans has been questioned, and political pressure has been brought to reduce, if not eliminate, our interaction with other animals. While this situation has directly affected all who use animals commercially, few have been more affected than scientists who use animals in their research. As a result, researchers have found it necessary to defend their use of animals.

The usual justification given for animal research is that the benefits of the research to humans outweighs the costs to the animals. However, this argument raises the question of how many animals we are justified in sacrificing in order to benefit ourselves. This question arises because the relationship between humans and animals is viewed as one-sided, with humans benefitting at the expense of animals. Indeed, so pervasive is this view that current U.S. government policy directs that the number of animals used in research be minimized and that alternatives to animal research be sought—with the implied goal of eventually ending animal research.

But is the use of animals in research (or, for that matter, for food and clothing) an exploitative relationship in which all of the benefits accrue to humans? In answering this question, it is important to realize that all living organisms have close relationships with others and that these rela-

Henry E. Heffner, "The Symbiotic Nature of Animal Research," *Perspectives in Biology and Medicine*, vol. 43, Autumn 1999. Copyright © 1999 by The Johns Hopkins University Press. Reproduced by permission.

tionships have been the subject of scientific study. Ironically, the knowledge gained from such studies has not been applied to the debate concerning the use of animals in science.

The purpose of this paper is to examine our use of animals in terms of what is known about the relationships between living organisms, particularly symbiotic relationships. In doing so, it is necessary to consider the general issue of domestication, of which animal research is a part, and to wexamine the use of the reproductive strategy known as kin selection. As will be seen, such an analysis leads to conclusions that have relevance to our use of animals.

Mutualism as a form of symbiosis

The term *symbiosis* was first used in 1879 by Anton de Bary, a German mycologist at the University of Strasbourg, to refer to the living together or close association of two different species. Although it sometimes has been used to refer to interactions in which both species (the symbionts) benefit, it is more commonly used in a broad sense to refer to all types of interactions. One form of symbiosis is *parasitism*, in which one symbiont obtains food and/or shelter at the expense of another, but without causing immediate death; indeed, it is the most common lifestyle found in nature. Examples include the various bacterial, viral, and other diseases that infect all organisms including humans. A second form is *commensalism*, in which one species obtains food and/or shelter from another at little cost (or benefit) to the host. The house mice and rats that consume small amounts of our food and the mites that live in our beds are not considered to be noticeably detrimental to our survival, although they occasionally may be so. However, it is *mutualism*, in which both parties benefit, that is of most relevance here. A prime example is our own bodies, for humans, like other mammals, are properly considered as complex organisms consisting of animal cells and bacteria; the bacteria that inhabit our gut not only outnumber the cells of our body, but constitute a complex ecosystem whose metabolic activity is on par with that of the liver and without which we could not survive.

> *It is clear that engaging in a mutualistic relationship with humans is an extraordinarily successful survival strategy for animals.*

The measure of benefit derived from a mutualistic relationship is the amount that the relationship has contributed to the reproductive success of both species and, conversely, has reduced the probability that either might become extinct. Species that are considered relatively resistant to extinction have the following characteristics: (1) they are quite numerous, with the result that a sudden reduction in their numbers will not reduce the population below the minimum necessary for survival (i.e., the minimum viable population); (2) they are geographically widespread, and thus can survive local environmental changes that may eliminate them from particular locales; and (3) they are phenotypically diverse, making them adaptable to new and changing environments. Thus, the success of a species can be estimated in terms of these three characteristics, which reflect the long-term probability that they will continue to pass on their DNA.

Domestication as a mutualistic relationship

The initial interaction of *Homo sapiens* with animals was a predator-prey relationship—we were usually the predator. Over 10,000 years ago, this relationship started to change as humans began to domesticate animals. The consequences were profound: not only did we gain reliable sources of food and clothing, but of power as well (e.g., horsepower). Along with the domestication of plants, the domestication of animals has made humans one of the more successful of extant mammals—not only have our numbers increased, but we have successfully invaded a wider variety of habitats as a result of domestication.

If humans have succeeded as a result of domestication, so have the animals we domesticated. Like humans, domestic animals have increased their numbers far beyond their wild ancestors, and they have spread to every continent on the globe. In addition, the diversification of domestic animals into numerous breeds has led to greater phenotypic variation than existed in the wild populations. In short, domestication is a mutualistic relationship that has made domestic animals far more successful and much more resistant to extinction than their wild ancestors, while simultaneously strengthening mankind's ability to survive.

> *Humans . . . protect domestic animals from the ravages of nature, and it is those animals that otherwise would not have survived that we use.*

An example of this benefit can be seen in the spread of domestic animals to North America as a result of European colonization. It has been remarked that during the early colonial period, domestic animals far outnumbered humans in the New World. They still do. The spread of domestic cattle provides a revealing illustration of this process.

Domestic cattle are bovids and belong to the subfamily Bovini, which includes the American bison. Interestingly, bison are so closely related to domestic cattle that they can interbreed and produce fertile offspring. Prior to the advent of European colonists (both human and animal), there were estimated to be 30 million bison in North America and, of course, no domestic cattle. Now the situation is reversed. Currently, there is only a remnant population of around 65,000 bison, but there are 140 million domestic cattle in North America and over 250 million more in South America. In other words, there are now far more Bovini in the New World than there were before the advent of domestic cattle. Moreover, the diversity of bovids has increased markedly—whereas there were previously only two or three varieties of bison, there are over 50 breeds of cattle. Thus, it is clear that engaging in a mutualistic relationship with humans is an extraordinarily successful survival strategy for animals—at least as long as there are humans.

Kin selection

Domestic cattle not only demonstrate the success of forming mutualistic relationships with humans, they also provide a clear example of a common strategy for perpetuating one's genes, namely, kin selection. Kin selection[1] is a strategy in which the ability of individuals to reproduce directly is reduced, either because their own lives are put at risk protecting their close relatives or because their individual reproductive efforts have been curtailed and their efforts directed instead to aiding the reproductive success of their close relatives. A common example of the former is a sentinel animal that gives warning calls of predators to protect others in its group, but at the risk of drawing the attention of the predator to itself. Examples of individuals that forego reproduction are found among social animals, the classic examples being eusocial insects, such as ants, bees, and termites, whose workers devote their efforts to caring for the offspring of the queen to whom they are closely related. A similar arrangement is found among mammals in colonies of naked mole rats (*Heterocephalus glaber*) where a single reproducing female (the "queen") suppresses the sexual development of the other females in the colony by excreting a hormone in her urine.

Two points should be noted. First, kin selection does not usually involve choice on the part of the individuals involved. Instead, it is a strategy imposed on them by natural selection—it persists because it is successful. Second, for kin selection to work, the genetic success of the "donor" [the animal that gives up its reproductive rights] must be greater than that which would result if it attempted to reproduce directly, and this can only occur if relinquishing direct reproductive efforts benefits an animal's close relatives more than others. Thus, the benefit to others must be in proportion to the degree of kinship with the donor and, among mammals, the closest relatives are parents and full siblings as well as offspring.

The role of humans in kin selection

Returning to the example of cattle, it can be seen that most individual animals do not have the opportunity to reproduce before they are slaughtered and thus do not contribute directly to their gene pool. However, they do have an indirect but powerful influence on the success of their genes.[2] As noted by Charles Darwin, we continue to breed closely related animals in order to perpetuate the desirable features of those that we use. Indeed, it has been stated [by authors Victor Rice and F.N. Andrews] that "the only sure test of an animal's breeding worth is the quality of its offspring." Thus, the selection of breeding stock is based not simply on the characteristics of the breeding animal itself, but on the characteristics of its offspring, with the result that offspring that exhibit desirable characteristics (e.g., rapid weight gain) increase the reproductive success of their parents and, most importantly, the success of their own genes. As a result, whereas kin selection plays a small role in wild cattle, as when members

1. This term refers to the evolution of traits that are passed on by the relatives of individuals that express the traits.   2. If an animal with valued traits is killed, humans protect its kin because those relatives may also carry the genes for desirable characteristics.

of a herd defend each other from predators, it has become a major mechanism for perpetuating the genes of domestic animals.

Humans benefit domestic animals

It should be noted that the increased use of kin selection by domestic animals has not necessarily changed their overall mortality rates (although their survivorship curves [the length of their lives] have changed as a result of human protection of newborn animals . . .). In the wild, first-year mortality rates for animals are typically 80 percent or higher, especially when the environment has reached its carrying capacity. Furthermore, among those animals that survive, the competition for a mate and resources to reproduce is so intense that many fail to breed successfully. Humans, however, protect domestic animals from the ravages of nature, and it is those animals that otherwise would not have survived that we use. Although the reproductive rates of domestic animals could be reduced, . . . this, of course, would eliminate their usefulness to us, and we would no longer have sufficient reason to continue our relationship with them.

Because [domestic animals] are now inextricably tied to us, anything that benefits us automatically benefits them and, conversely, anything that threatens our survival is a threat to theirs.

Whether in the wild or in association with humans, the death rate in a stable population will be the same—it will equal the birth rate (assuming equal immigration and emigration rates). However, the death of an animal in the wild from starvation, predation, or disease is wasted effort on the part of the parents, in that it contributes nothing to the perpetuation of their genes. The death of an animal for human use, on the other hand, contributes to its genetic success by encouraging us to protect its genetic line [lest its desirable traits be lost]. Thus it should be clear that the only losers in this relationship are the predators and parasites that attack animals in the wild.

Animals are dependent on humans

The use of animals in research is another example of mutualism in which the same points regarding domestication and kin selection apply. Most species commonly used in research had already established relationships with us before they expanded into the laboratory. Laboratory mice and rats are recent descendants of wild house mice (*Mus musculus*) and Norway rats (*Rattus norvegicus*) that evolved as commensals to live in our houses and feed off our stores of grain. Similarly, dogs are scavengers and are believed to have begun their relationship with us by feeding off our garbage and wastes—as they still do in parts of Africa and the Middle East. Indeed, the coprophagic habits of dogs were well known to polar explorers, who depended on sled dogs, and are still familiar to dog owners with children in diapers. The domestic cat entered into a mutualistic relationship with us by eating the wild rodents that feed on our grain. Thus, even before becoming domesticated, mice, rats, cats, and dogs were already dependent on humans for their survival.

A new niche

During the latter half of the 19th century, it became apparent that the use of animals in research would greatly expand our knowledge of medicine and physiology. This was made apparent by research on animal diseases, such as anthrax and rabies, that helped establish the fact that microorganisms (germs) can cause disease. Indeed, up until that time, the medical community had overwhelmingly rejected the germ theory of disease. It was the application of the animal research of [Louis] Pasteur and others that led surgeons to begin washing their hands before, instead of after, surgery. At about the same time, animals were used in increasing numbers as physiological research began to expand.

The movement of animals into the laboratory represents their expansion into a new ecological niche. In the case of mice and rats, their relationship with us has been elevated from commensalism to mutualism. Because we now breed them, both their numbers and genetic diversity have increased to the point that there are now well over 200 stocks and strains of laboratory rodents. Indeed, the fact that the various types of laboratory mice and rats are reproductively isolated from each other and have diverged genetically may justify considering them as new species. . . . The fact that humans are responsible for their reproductive isolation is yet another illustration of the well-established principle that one species can affect the evolution of another (compare for example, the coevolution of flowering plants and the insects that pollinate them).

To restrict our acquisition of knowledge by reducing the use of animals in research is not in the best interests of the animals involved.

Some animals, such as cats and dogs, had already established mutualistic relationships with us, and their movement into the laboratory represents an expansion of this relationship. Other animals, such as macaques and chimpanzees, have no closer relationship with us outside the laboratory. However, chimpanzees are currently in danger of becoming extinct, and the best chance for their survival may be to establish a mutualistic relationship with us, i.e., to become domesticated. Thus, one obvious survival strategy for chimpanzees would be to expand their use of kin selection and, capitalizing on their genetic similarity with humans become essential to medical research, thus increasing their own ability to survive—as well as ours.

Animals are benefited by their use in research

Regardless of whether the use of previously domesticated animals in research results in a significant increase in their numbers, they benefit from our research in an indirect, but important way. Domestic animals have developed a dependence on humans no less extreme than the dependence of flowering plants on insects. Because they are now inextricably tied to us, anything that benefits us automatically benefits them and, conversely, anything that threatens our survival is a threat to theirs. For the moment, humans have what appears to be a relatively secure position on this planet. We have achieved this through the use of our intellect, which has allowed us to stabilize our food supply, develop new sources of energy, and hold many diseases at bay (few diseases have actually been eliminated). However history teaches us that all species eventually become extinct, and the best we can hope for is to delay this inevitability as long as possible. Thus, to restrict our acquisition of knowledge by reducing the use of animals in research is not in the best interest of the animals involved—not only because it decreases a laboratory species' usefulness to us and shuts it out of an ecological niche, but because it reduces the survivability of their major symbiotic partner, us.

At worst, the laboratory environment may sometimes be as harsh as life in the wild.

If research animals benefit from their mutualistic interactions with humans, why would anyone think that these interactions are exploitative and should be discontinued? Although the answers are usually based on personal philosophical principles, there are two points that can be addressed objectively. These are: that life in a laboratory is inferior to that in the wild, and that humans would never accept a similar type of relationship. Both of these points merit scrutiny.

Laboratory life is better

The first point is based on the observation that most research animals are not given the opportunity to reproduce, that they are euthanized before they reach senescence, and that they live in environments (laboratories) that differ from their wild habitats. But is the laboratory environment inferior to that found in the wild? As previously noted, animals in the wild suffer high mortality rates, are subject to starvation, predation, and disease, and many, if not most, fail to breed successfully. It would appear that, at worst, the laboratory environment may sometimes be as harsh as life in the wild—for example, when animals are infected in order to study a disease, although even these animals do not have to worry about finding food and shelter or avoiding predators while they are ill. But the fact that animals in captivity live healthier and, in many cases, longer lives than their wild counterparts demonstrates that it is, in fact, a better environment.

Along this line, it should be noted that the natural habitat of animals bred for research is the laboratory—laboratory mice and rats are incapable of surviving in the wild. That they require us to survive does not make them "degenerate" any more than flowering plants that require insects for pollination are degenerate. Thus, animals bred for research are properly viewed as animals that have successfully invaded the laboratory niche, relying heavily on kin selection to perpetuate their genes. Similarly, wild animals brought into the laboratory (or other human environments, such as a zoo) can be viewed as animals exploring a new ecological niche. Interestingly, a mutualistic relationship may develop between humans and wild animals without us directly breeding them. This is because a demand for a wild species may lead to a commercial interest in perpetuating it by maintaining its wild habitat—a classic example being the maintenance of habitats by sportsmen. Thus, we seem to have an inherent tendency to elevate our interactions with other animals to one of mutualism, and our desire to save endangered animals from extinction may be due in part to a desire to hold open the possibility of future mutualistic interactions with them.

Necessary sacrifices

The second argument against our use of animals is that we would not accept a similar relationship in which some humans would have to suffer in order for others to benefit, and that it is therefore unethical to impose such a relationship on animals. However, we do accept such relationships. While we would like all members of our species to live long and productive lives, we constantly compromise by sacrificing some for the benefit of others—a common example being the altruistic actions of soldiers in time of war. However, a much more common (and largely overlooked) example of sacrifice is our use of the automobile.

In the United States, about 30,000 people are killed each year in accidents involving passenger vehicles. Moreover, automobiles, like animal predators, tend to be inefficient, and over 1.5 million disabling injuries can be attributed to such accidents. Yet no one has had the temerity to seriously propose abolishing the automobile and forcing people to use much safer public transportation (or restricting travel altogether, which would save even more lives). If we accept for ourselves the principle that some must inevitably suffer so that others can enjoy the advantages of private transportation, then should we deny animals the opportunity to make a similar arrangement in order to ensure their very survival?

There is, however, one ethical principle that can be used in evaluating our relationships with animals. It is simply to ask whether we are providing them with a better situation than they would encounter in the wild, i.e., whether we are giving them a "better deal." There are examples of human-animal interactions in which the answer to this question is obviously no—for example, a predator-prey interaction in which animals are hunted to extinction. Domestication, on the other hand, is clearly an interaction in which animals are more successful than they are in the wild. In short, the use of animals by humans, whether it be for the accumulation of knowledge through research or any other reason, typically causes us to work to ensure the continuation of their genetic lines. And that, after all, is the purpose of life.

7

Organ Transplants Between Species Violate Animals' Rights

Dan Lyons

Dan Lyons is a specialist in the ethics of animal transplantation. He is also director of the animal rights group Uncaged Campaigns. This organization is best known for uncovering and winning a legal battle to release animal experimentation reports of Huntingdon Life Sciences, a commercial research company that Uncaged Campaigns accuses of breaching animal welfare practices.

In xenotransplantation, live organs, tissues, or cells from one animal are inserted into an animal of a different species. Scientists hope that as a result of this research animal organs can one day be transplanted into humans whose organs are failing. These experiments, however, cause unnecessary animal suffering. Animals are dismembered in bizarre transplantations, administered experimental drugs, and subjected to extreme physical and psychological suffering, which goes unnoticed by regulatory agencies.

X enotransplantation is the transplantation of live organs, tissues or cells between different species. Such transplants are also referred to as *xenografts*.

This report organises and interprets an extensive cache of leaked documents that afford an extraordinary and unique insight into arguably the most controversial programme of animal experimentation in the United Kingdom in modern times: xenotransplantation research. The material includes 39 draft reports describing xenotransplantation experiments on higher primates commissioned by the UK biotechnology company Imutran Ltd and conducted by Huntingdon Life Sciences [HLS] at their Cambridgeshire laboratories. Other documents include correspondence, meeting minutes, feasibility studies and internal reports concerning many aspects of the conduct of and plans for xenotransplantation research.

The experiments have predominantly involved the transplantation of hearts and kidneys from genetically-engineered pigs into two species of higher primates, baboons and cynomolgus monkeys. Following transplantation, the primates have been administered experimental cocktails of drugs in an effort to suppress their immune systems and thus prevent rejection of the pig organs. Through conducting this research, Imutran, the Cambridge-based biotechnology subsidiary of the multinational drug firm Novartis, hope to develop a package of treatments consisting of transgenic [genetically modified] pig organs and accompanying immunosuppressive therapies to sell through health care providers to patients with malfunctioning organs.

Controversial research

Quite apart from the revelations of the acquired documents, xenotransplantation research has been controversial because:

- If xenotransplantation ever proved successful, the use of genetically-modified pigs as sources of organs would signify a novel form of suffering, exploitation and death deliberately inflicted by human society on nonhuman animals.
- The extensive use of higher primates in procedures that have caused very high levels of suffering.
- Complex species differences between nonhuman primates and human beings that render results gained by experiments on the former unreliable as a guide to the human situation.
- The contracting of this research programme to Huntingdon Life Sciences, a commercial research company whose track record includes breaches of animal welfare and Good Laboratory Practice (GLP) regulations.
- The profoundly difficult problems faced in trying to overcome the rejection of pig organs by the human immune system.
- Serious doubts exist about the physiological and biochemical compatibility of pig organs with the human body.
- The potential of xenotransplantation to introduce novel infectious organisms such as retroviruses into the human population, thereby causing new pandemics with echoes of HIV/AIDS.
- The existence of alternative methods of tackling the health problems of organ failure such as preventative health measures, increasing the pool of human donors, mechanical devices or growing new organs from human cells.
- The distributive justice of xenotransplantation: whether it represents the most efficient and most equitable use of scarce health resources.
- The commercial motivation behind the research, which adds up to an attempt to dominate a market that is predicted to be worth $11 billion by 2010.

Psychological damage

Another controversial element of Imutran's xenotransplantation research centres on the housing conditions of transgenic pigs. The acquired information does not focus on the procedures affecting pigs, apart from descriptions in the study reports of their dismemberment and killing in order to derive organs for experimental transplantation into the primates. Nonetheless, it is important to note the impact that xenotransplantation is having on these animals. In order to minimise the risk of the transgenic pigs acquiring any pathogens which could then be passed on to future recipients of xenografts, the pigs are kept in what is known as Qualified Pathogen Free (QPF) conditions. Pigs are highly intelligent, complex and sociable animals. When given the opportunity under natural conditions, they will spend some 75% of their daylight hours in rooting, foraging and exploratory activities. QPF conditions require a relatively barren, indoor environment that will deprive pigs of the chance to satisfy adequately their desire to explore and forage, leading to behaviours indicative of psychological suffering such as stereotypical behaviour and aggression. Indeed, an undercover investigation has discovered fighting among Imutran's pigs. In a letter to Uncaged Campaigns, the RSPCA [Royal Society for the Prevention of Cruelty to Animals] has stated:

> The RSPCA has always expressed extremely serious concern at the welfare implications of keeping pigs in QPF [and other similar] conditions. We believe that this seriously curtails one of the Five Freedoms widely recognised as important for farm animals.

Additionally, the RSPCA responded to the Kennedy Report [by the government-appointed Advisory Group on the Ethics of Xenotransplantation] by submitting:

> The RSPCA is seriously concerned that the recommendation relating to the maintenance of animals in biosecure conditions will result in environmentally sterile and barren accommodation.

Requirements for the surgical derivation of piglets and their early weaning also lead to distress for both mother sow and piglet. Source piglets will be weaned as young as 5 to 7 days, an acknowledged breach of the Welfare of Livestock Regulations 1994. The Home Office, however, condones this to facilitate the development of xenotransplantation.

Evidence of animal suffering

The hitherto secret information presented via this report confirms and intensifies these fears, particularly in terms of the intense suffering of primates and the implausibility of viable xenotransplantation. Additionally, new concerns are raised about the standards of laboratory practice during the studies and the extent to which the Home Office has fulfilled its duty to enforce regulations pertaining to animal experiments and limits on the suffering of animals.

The true extent of the suffering inflicted on higher primates is now revealed—from capture and/or captive breeding in the tropics . . . on through highly stressful and sometimes lethal long-distance transportation in close confinement . . . ending with the extreme torment of the xenotransplantation experiments themselves. The following clinical observations, recorded in the acquired study reports, are a snapshot of the misery endured by hundreds of primates at the hands of HLS and Imutran. The first notes are for the last two days in the life of baboon W205m, who died in a study involving the transplantation of transgenic pig hearts into the necks of wild-caught baboons:

20	am	Quiet but alert. Scab on operation site appears clean and dry. Keeps holding area where transplanted heart is.
	pm	Quiet and huddled. Little movement and unsteady when moving. Showing signs of discomfort.
21	am	Quiet and huddled. Scab on operation site appears dry. Reluctant to move. Marked firm swelling around implant. Animal showing obvious discomfort. Fluid swelling developing in sub-mandibular region.
	pm	Sero-sanguinous fluid drained but no purulent material. Transplanted heart beat barely palpable. Swelling so large animal sacrificed for humane reasons.

And these clinical signs relate to a cynomolgus monkey T397m, into whose abdomen a transgenic pig kidney was transplanted:

21	am	Quiet, huddled on perch, reluctant to move. No reaction to external stimuli, vacant appearance. Clear nasal discharge. Liquid faeces in cage.
	pm	Quiet, huddled on perch, reluctant to move. No reaction to external stimuli, vacant appearance. Clear nasal discharge. Liquid faeces in cage. Collapsed following administration of parenteral dosing. Some recovery, very quiet, sitting holding perch. Little interest in surroundings.
22	am	Quiet and huddled. Reluctant to move. Constant grinding of teeth. Liquid faeces.

Additionally, over a quarter of the animals died on the operating table or within a few days because of technical failures in the surgical procedures.

Lack of progress

In 1995, Imutran predicted that the first human trials of their transgenic pig organs would take place the following year. But despite an intensive research effort that has sacrificed hundreds of higher primates and thousands of pigs, the goal of achieving viable xenotransplantation remains as remote as ever. The development of the particular line of transgenic organs that Imutran have been testing for five years—known as hDAF—appears to be in crisis, with Novartis setting an 18 month time limit (from April 2000) for achieving a quantum leap in survival times.

In order to try and attain this progress, this spring (2000) Imutran appear to have abandoned primate research in the UK and, instead, are coordinating the activities of a group of external collaborators. One of the

US collaborations . . . was set up in 1999 "following the selection of first potential sites for clinical trials in the US.". . . .

Study risks and errors

The possibility of risks to public health are raised by the involvement of human transplant surgeons in experiments on wild-caught baboons who appear to have been carrying the potentially lethal Simian Herpes B virus. . . .

Another feature of the evidence contained in the acquired documents relates to the manner in which the studies were performed. On several occasions Imutran expressed dissatisfaction with the level of service provided by Huntingdon Life Sciences, claiming in one instance that some studies exhibited "a fundamental shortfall in GLP compliance." Throughout the research programme, we estimate that 520 separate data recording errors and failures occurred. The illegal re-use of a group of monkeys took place at HLS. The most heated criticism arose from two incidents that took place within a month of each other in winter 98/99. Firstly, a monkey was accidentally given a quadruple overdose of an immunosuppressant drug—she died the next day. Secondly, a vital blood sample was taken at completely the wrong time, thereby hindering attempts by Imutran to calculate the optimum dose of immunosuppressant drugs.

Imutran themselves do not appear to be blameless. Seven baboons appear to have been transplanted without a crucial antibody reading being taken before the surgeries. On another occasion, a monkey died four days after being vivisected because of a swab left inside him that caused his spleen to go septic. In another accident, a piglet kidney due to be transplanted into a monkey was frozen and thus rendered useless, leading to the monkey being killed while under anaesthetic in preparation for the transplant. Later on, several discrepancies in the pathology reports for a group of primates leads [an employee of] Imutran to comment that the company's attainment of international quality management standards (ISO9000) was in jeopardy.

The failures and omissions may have compromised animal welfare in certain instances, and generally they had the potential to undermine the reliability and usefulness of the data generated by the experiments. The latest documents reveal that Imutran have "severe problems" with the state of the data from these studies. Given the intense suffering inflicted on primates and the costs in terms of the lives of the primates and the pigs, the very least one should expect from this research project is that the studies produce optimum quantity and quality of information.

Regulation failures

The documents reveal the Home Office's failure to enforce the regulatory framework for animal research. In the first instance, the severe and prolonged suffering of many animals potentially breaks absolute limits enshrined in British and European legislation that are supposed to outlaw such extreme distress. Secondly, the Home Office must apply a cost-benefit assessment to decide whether to permit a programme of animal experimentation. This formula is a central feature of the legislation governing animal experimentation in the UK. However, the costs inflicted on animals in the course of xenotransplantation research appear to far outweigh any reasonable assessment of the benefits likely to accrue.

The Home Office decided to re-issue Huntingdon Life Sciences (HLS) with a new Certificate of Designation in 1997. In re-issuing the Certificate, the Home Office accepted that HLS had satisfied 16 conditions which were designed to prevent incidents of malpractice at the company, some of which were exposed by an undercover investigation broadcast on Channel Four in March 1997. This new evidence casts doubt on the basis of the Home Office's decision. For example, just one month after the Home Office had given a new Certificate to HLS, a group of monkeys were illegally re-used in experiments at the establishment. This breach of the law should have been prevented by the implementation of the improvements that formed the 16 conditions laid down by the Home Office that HLS should have fulfilled to retain a Certificate of Designation—but the Home Office did not revoke HLS' Certificate in the light of these illegal procedures. Errors and omissions in the conduct of the studies also took place during the period when HLS were said to be in the process of meeting the 16 conditions, and directly afterwards (e.g. the illegal re-use incident).

Following transplantation, the primates have been administered experimental cocktails of drugs in an effort to suppress their immune systems and thus prevent rejection of the pig organs.

Other incidents of regulatory inaction included the response to the deaths of three cynomolgus monkeys during transit from the Philippines to HLS for xenotransplantation research: the crates that held the monkeys had broken regulations on size and ventilation. In one confirmed instance, the journey time for an importation of wild-caught baboons was considerably longer than the estimate submitted on Imutran's application form. The Home Office appears to have asked for some assurance from Imutran that the same baboons, who arrived in May 1999, would be used relatively quickly in recognition of the suffering imposed on them by the laboratory environment. However, the animals languished at HLS for at least seven months. Additionally, other wild-caught baboons imported previously had been incarcerated for up to two years in conditions that appear to have been inferior to those experienced by the May 1999 contingent.

Automatic approval

The following sentence to emerge from the minutes of a meeting at Imutran is revealing: "[The local Home Office Inspector for Imutran] has on several occasions expressed his view that the new License will be approved before the existing license is revoked and that Thursday [i.e., a meeting of the Animal Procedures Committee (APC)—the government's advisory committee—to discuss the licence application] will be merely a 'rubber stamping' exercise."

In the context of the relationship between the Home Office and Imutran, another significant comment came from [an employee of] Imutran as he outlined the points to emerge from a company meeting that took place towards the beginning of the primate vivisection programme in spring 1995:

"[An employee] of Imutran agreed to talk to [an Inspector] at the Home Office re technical failures, life-supporting heart in baboon and to generally chew the cud and ensure smooth and rapid passage of forthcoming 19b. application. Important that [the inspector] understands the issues (technical difficulty, imminence, etc.) and will give us upward support of the application for orthotopic work. We have to work to make him look like a jolly good bureaucrat and yet achieve our goals as well!"

Public interest

The justification for publishing these confidential documents arises from the right of the public to know the full facts of this hugely significant research programme. . . .

The victims of this research have been the higher primates and the pigs. The "public interest" is not the only legitimate interest in this affair, a point confirmed—ironically—by the stipulation in the Animals (Scientific Procedures) Act 1986 that the interests of animals should be taken into account in determining whether to licence vivisection procedures. A true democracy reflects the principle that those affected by decisions must have an input—where necessary, voiced by an advocate—into the decision-making process. Thus the interests of nonhuman animals have a vital role to play in democratic government, particularly when policies affecting their interests are being formulated and executed.

Lastly, there is a clear public interest in the ethical issue of how our society treats nonhuman animals. Moral responsibility and public debates seeking to ascertain the nature of such responsibilities are inescapable aspects of the human condition. They define who we are and how we value and feel about ourselves and our society. A significant proportion of the public do take a deep interest in the treatment of animals.

8

Organ Transplants Between Species Are Ethical

The Pontifical Academy for Life

The Pontifical Academy for Life, a Catholic group composed of pope-appointed academicians from different branches of biomedical sciences, researches problems concerning the promotion and defense of life.

Xenotransplantation, the transplantation of organs, tissues, or cells from one species to another, is not unethical. The Bible affirms that God created animals to serve humans, and humans may use animals, wisely and responsibly, for the good of humanity. Therefore, sacrificing animals in xenotransplantation research is justified, provided that an ethics committee reviews every procedure to determine that unnecessary animal suffering is prevented, the number of animals used is limited, and the experiment is necessary and reasonable.

Besides the scientific and technical aspects of xenotransplantation, . . . anthropological and ethical considerations are also involved. The purpose of this [viewpoint] is to explore these considerations, albeit by way of a brief overview.

In addition to the problems raised by every transplant, it seems to us that there are . . . issues specifically related to xenotransplantation: the acceptability of man's intervening in the order of the creation [and] the ethical feasibility of using animals to improve the chances for survival and well-being of human beings. . . .

Human intervention in animals' lives

To begin with, we would like to deal briefly with a fundamental question that, generally, is posed by the different religious traditions, albeit with different accents: this concerns the possibility itself that man may licitly intervene in the realities that exist in the universe in general and, more particularly, in those things that concern animals.

In view of the more specifically theological nature of such a question, we deem it useful to offer a short summary of the Catholic position on

The Pontifical Academy for Life, *Prospects for Xenotransplantation*. Vatican City: Vatican, November 28, 2001, Special Supplement Pages I–VIII.

47

this question, applying the language and the methods proper to theological anthropology.

By what right can humans, whom God created as female and male, and whose full human dignity must be recognized at every stage of life, intervene in the created order, perhaps even modifying some of its aspects? What criteria must be adopted and what limitations must be introduced?

From imagery of the account of creation "in six days", it is evident that God established a hierarchy of values among the various creatures. Moreover, this hierarchy also emerges from a rational consideration of the transcendent richness and dignity of the human person.

The service of animals to man represents a totally new application in xenotransplantation.

Man, created "in the image and likeness of God", is placed at the centre and at the summit of the created order, not only because everything that exists is intended for him, but also because woman and man have the task of co-operating with the Creator in leading creation to its final perfection. "Be fruitful and multiply, and fill the earth and subdue it" (Gen 1: 28): this is the mandate that God gives to human beings, "dominion" over the created order, in his name. In this regard, Pope John Paul II writes in his encyclical *"Laborem Exercens"*: "Man is the image of God partly through the mandate received from his Creator to subdue, to dominate, the earth. In carrying out this mandate, man, every human being, reflects the very action of the Creator of the universe".

Responsible use of animals

This, therefore, is the deepest meaning of the action of man in relation to the created universe: certainly not that of arbitrarily "lording it over" the other creatures, reducing them to humiliating and destructive slavery in order to satisfy any whim that he may have, but to guide, through his responsible work, the life of the creation towards the authentic and integral good of man (the *whole* man and *every* man).

Certain documents of the Second Vatican Council had already affirmed this truth. In *"Lumen Gentium"*, for example, we read: "Therefore, by their competence in secular disciplines and by their activity, interiorly raised up by grace, they (the laity) must work earnestly in order that created goods through human labor, technical skill and civil culture may serve the utility of all men according to the plan of the Creator and the light of his Word. May these goods be more suitably distributed among all men and in their own way may they be conducive to universal progress, in human and Christian liberty". Also the decree of the Second Vatican Council on the apostolate of the laity takes up this idea when it asserts that "this natural goodness of theirs (of the realities that make up the temporal order) receives an added dignity from their relation with the human person, for whose use they have been created".

In summary, therefore, there should be a reaffirmation of the right and duty of man, according to the mandate from his Creator and never against the natural order established by him, to act within the created order and on the created order, making use as well, of other creatures, in order to achieve the final goal of all creation: the glory of God and the full and definitive bringing about of His Kingdom, through the promotion of man. The words of St. Irenaeus of Lyons still ring out with all their truth: "Living man is the glory of God and man's life is the vision of God".

The use of animals in xenotransplantation

For a theological reflection that will help to formulate an ethical assessment on the practice of xenotransplantation, we do well to consider what the intention of the Creator was in bringing animals into existence. Since they are creatures, animals have their own specific value which man must recognize and respect. However, God placed them, together with the other nonhuman creatures, at the service of man, so that man could achieve his overall development also through them.

It should be noted that this role of "service" rendered to man by other creatures occurs in different ways according to the cultural advances of humanity. Limiting ourselves to scientific and technological progress in the biomedical field, the service of animals to man represents a totally new application in xenotransplantation, which, therefore, in principle is not in conflict with the order of the creation. On the contrary, xenotransplantation represents for man a further opportunity for creative responsibility in making reasonable use of the power that God has given to him.

Furthermore, even if one limits oneself to a purely rational analysis, without desiring to make use of theological reasoning, one can reach the same conclusions on a practical level.

A simple look at humanity's long presence on the earth is sufficient to show an irrefutable fact clearly: it is man who has always directed the realities of the world, controlling the other living and non-living beings according to determined purposes. It is moreover in its relationship with man that the axiological measure (moral value) of every existing reality is revealed in a universal harmonic and orderly design that indicates all the fullness of the sense of reality.

> *The sacrifice of animals can be justified only if required to achieve an important benefit for man, as is the case with xenotransplantation.*

In particular, man has always made use of animals for his primary needs (food, work, clothing, etc.) in a sort of natural "cooperation" that has constantly marked the different stages of progress and the development of civilization.

Such a position of "excellence" is a witness to and also demonstrates the ontological superiority of mankind over the other beings of the earth; this superiority is founded on the very nature of the human person, whose rational and spiritual dimensions place man at the centre of the universe, so that he may use its existing resources (including animals) in a wise and responsible manner, seeking the authentic promotion of every being.

The relationship between man and animals

To analyse more deeply the point under discussion, two issues of an ethical nature must be addressed. First, there is the question of the use of animals in order to improve man's chances of survival or to improve his health: the obvious starting point here is the particular way in which one views the relationship between man and animals. Second, there is the question of the acceptability of breaching the barrier between animal species and the human species.

With regard to the first issue, contemporary thinking includes two opposing and extreme viewpoints. There are those who believe that animals and man have equal dignity and those who believe that animals are totally at the mercy of man. In the former case, the use of animals is seen as species-ism or tyranny of man over animals. Even reducing human suffering could not justify the use of animals unless the contrary possibility was also allowed. In the latter case, man can use animals arbitrarily without being limited by ethical considerations.

From our point of view, supported by the biblical perspective that asserts, as stated above, that man is created "in the image and likeness of God" (cf. Gen 1: 26–27), we reaffirm that humans have a *unique* and *higher* dignity. However, humans must also answer to the Creator for the manner in which they treat animals. As a consequence, the sacrifice of animals can be justified only if required to achieve an important benefit for man, as is the case with xenotransplantation of organs or tissues to man, even when this involves experiments on animals and/or genetically modifying them.

Ethical requirements

However, even in this case, there is the ethical requirement that in using animals, man must observe certain conditions: unnecessary animal suffering must be prevented; criteria of real necessity and reasonableness must be respected; genetic modifications that could significantly alter the biodiversity and the balance of the species in the animal world must be avoided.

The theological and moral point of view sees no substantial problem in the utilization of different animal species (nonhuman primates or non-primates), but leaves open the question of differing levels of sensibilities between animals of different species and that of equilibrium among species and within a species.

The point should also be made that Catholic theology does not have preclusions, on a religious or ritual basis, in using any animal as a source of organs or tissues for transplantation to man. . . .

The use of organs from engineered animals for xenotransplantation raises the need for certain reflections on transgenesis and its ethical implications.

The ethics of using transgenic animals

The term "transgenic animal" is used to indicate an animal whose genetic make-up has been modified by the introduction of a new gene (or genes). In contrast, the term "knock out" is used to designate those animals in which a given endogenous gene (or genes) is no longer expressed. In either case, such animals will express particular characteristics which will be transmitted to the offspring.

As we have already observed, the possibility of working out such genetic modifications, using genes of human origin as well, is morally acceptable when done in respect for the animal and for biodiversity, and with a view to bringing significant benefits to man himself. Therefore, while recognizing that *transgenesis* does not compromise the overall genetic identity of the mutated animal or its species, and reaffirming man's responsibility towards the created order and towards the pursuit of improving health by means of certain types of genetic manipulation, we will now enumerate some fundamental ethical conditions which must be respected:

1. Concern for the well-being of genetically modified animals should be guaranteed so that . . . possible modification of the anatomical, physiological and/or behavioural aspects of the animal may be assessed, all the while limiting the levels of stress and pain, suffering and anxiety experienced by the animal;

2. The effects on the offspring and possible repercussions for the environment should be considered;

3. Such animals should be kept under tight control and should not be released into the general environment;

4. The number of animals used in experiments should be kept to a bare minimum;

5. The removal of organs and/or tissues must take place during a single surgical operation;

6. Every experimental protocol on animals must be evaluated by a competent ethics committee. . . .

We conclude this document with the sincere hope that the effort made on this study by those who have participated in it—scientists, jurists, theologians and bioethicists—will represent a concrete contribution to the development of the discussion on the important theme of xenotransplantation. May it also be seen as a further expression of the close attention which the Catholic Church pays on problems related to human disease and suffering.

9

Cloning Animals Is Cruel

Philip Cohen

Philip Cohen is the bureau chief of the San Francisco office of New Scientist *magazine.*

Cloning causes immense suffering for the animals used in these experiments and their surrogate mothers. Most clones die young, and many of those that survive experience painful physical defects and decreased mental capacity. In addition, several surrogate mothers have died during pregnancy.

Zita the supercow was a beast in a million, the highest-ranked Holstein in the US. In her prime her milk yield was nearly twice the average, and cattle breeders paid top dollar to get her genes into their herds. Then, alas, she got old and died.

But dry your eyes. This is the age of the clone, and the genetic blueprints of prize cows can now be saved from the grave. Grazing on a farm in Maryland are Zita-2 and Zita-3, two three-month-old calves cloned using two cells from Zita's ears.

American cloning companies are busy making multiple copies of just about every top pedigree cow and bull in the land. In time, they hope identical supercows and superbulls will be bred, milked and even butchered for profit, just like the old ones. "We're cloning some of the highest-level bulls and think we can sell hundreds," says Ron Gillespie of Cyagra, the Massachusetts company that cloned Zita. For prize breeding animals, which can fetch $40,000 or more, cloning is economic even at today's going rate of $15,000 to $25,000 per cow. And as more animals are cloned, the cheaper it will get. "Push the price down to $10,000 and there would be 100,000 animals that it would be economic to clone, and in the $5000 range, millions."

That's millions of cloned cows and bulls. Created just to make food. In the US alone.

Ever since Dolly the sheep [the first successfully cloned mammal] was born, fears about cloning have been tempered by hopes that the technology will one day save thousands of human lives. And so it might. Already cloning is enabling scientists to produce animals capable of secreting valuable drugs in their milk, and to look for ways to clone tissues for transplantation. But developing these medical spin-offs could take up to 10 years. Cloned beef steaks and milkshakes could be with us much sooner.

So far, it's the baby cloners who have been in the firing line. Now, as companies like Cyagra forge ahead, the prospect of cows being cloned en masse for food is provoking alarm as well. And not just among animal welfare campaigners.

Ian Wilmut, the scientist who led the Dolly team, says it is vital that controlled farm trials of cattle cloning are carried out before any commercial production of cloned meat and dairy food is allowed. Companies need to prove that large-scale farm cloning involves no undue animal cruelty, that clones are as healthy as ordinary animals, and that food from cloned animals and their offspring is as safe and nutrious as conventional food, Wilmut told *New Scientist*. The cattle cloners "ought to be making systematic comparisons between clones and animals produced by embryo transfer, looking not just at their milk yield but also their health and lifespan". Until then, he says cloned food ought to be banned from shops and restaurants. "If companies start marketing this food and there are problems it will bring the whole technology into disrepute."

An animal welfare disaster

Herds of identical cloned animals would be a welfare disaster, says Joyce da Silva of Compassion in World Farming. "There would be a huge loss of genetic diversity with unforeseeable results in terms of animal illness."

A more immediate fear is that four years on from Dolly, cloning is still a waste of animal life. For every Zita-2 or Zita-3, say scientists at the sharp end, scores of clones die in the womb or develop deformities, and even clones that look healthy could be "ticking timebombs" destined to go awry.

> *[The calf's] lungs had never properly inflated, it had an enlarged heart, and its liver, which should have been a smooth crimson organ, was a roughened orange slab.*

Until recently, the full extent of the problem was hidden, largely because the cloned animals that don't survive don't get much space in scientific papers. A rare exception is a 1999 paper that appeared in the journal *Theriogenology* (vol 51, p 1451) under the heading "Clinical and pathological features of cloned transgenic calves and fetuses". The paper is an eye-opener.

Take the short life of "calf 1". Its placenta was bloated with six times the fluid of a normal pregnancy. Yet at birth it appeared normal. It mooed, started breathing and tried to stand. But appearances were deceptive. Its blood oxygen levels were one-third of what was expected, and carbon dioxide was up to three times normal. A day later, oxygen was pumped into its lungs and it was sedated with valium, but to no avail. The calf was soon dead. Its lungs had never properly inflated, it had an enlarged heart, and its liver, which should have been a smooth crimson organ, was a roughened orange slab.

Every fourth clone born is either stillborn or suffers from a lethal defect.

And those, remark some cloners wryly, were the "good old days". "We saw consistent defects, so we thought we'd find consistent solutions," says Jim Robi of the Massachusetts-based company Hematech. Oversized calves, lung and heart problems were the major themes. But now the more cloners you talk to, the longer the list of defects you hear about: enlarged tongues, squashed faces, bad kidneys, intestinal blockages, immune deficiencies, diabetes and shortened tendons that twist the young animal's feet into useless curves. "There's no pattern," says Robi. "It's perplexing."

Nor are the clones the only victims. The cow that carried calf 1 suffered a fatal fall in blood pressure after the birth. In fact, 4 of 12 surrogate mothers in the study died from pregnancy complications. Such deaths still happen despite improvements to cloning, says Michael Bishop of Wisconsin-based cloning company Infigen. "We sacrifice the cow and the clone . . . all the heroics in the world can't rescue those animals."

Low success rate

Despite this, some commercial cloners claim that cloning is no more wasteful than cattle breeders' standard artificial insemination methods. The figures to date suggest otherwise. While artificial insemination has a 40 per cent success rate, at best only 5 to 10 per cent of implanted cloned embryos become live calves. Around 75 per cent die in the first two months of pregnancy but miscarriages and terminations happen right to the end. And every fourth clone born is either stillborn or suffers from a lethal defect.

Even clones that survive and look healthy may harbour subtle defects. When Jon Hill from Cornell University examined the behaviour of newborn cow clones, he found they scored lower on average than typical cows in tests of attentiveness and intelligence. And mouse cloners say that one in three clones born looking normal become massively overweight a few weeks later. "Researchers who study obesity in mice say they have never seen such fat animals," says Ryuzo Yanagimachi of the University of Hawaii at Manoa.

Yanagimachi's team is now taking a close look at gene activity in newborn mouse clones. And things aren't looking good. "All cloned babies have some sort of errors," he says. "I'm surprised they can survive it."

Of course in some species, they don't survive at all—witness the countless failed attempts to get cloned cat and dog embryos to develop into living, breathing animals.

The cloning companies respond

Back at the cloning companies, scientists see this outbreak of negativity as little more than propaganda orchestrated to put off the baby cloners.

What happens with mice is no guide to what happens in other animals, insists Robert Lanza of Advanced Cell Technology in Worcester, Massachusetts. Lanza says his company has carried out fresh, and as yet unpublished, tests on virtually every surviving cow it has cloned and claims they are healthy and normal. "People have said they don't believe there is a single normal clone alive. That is just total nonsense."

In any case, say the cattle cloners, even if clones are quite different from other animals, that doesn't make them unhealthy. Infigen has amassed a huge database of blood tests from apparently healthy cloned cows. "The data suggested to the vets that some of them should be dead," says Infigen's Michael Bishop. "I think that shows we don't really know what normal is."

Perhaps. But whether that is the sort of reassurance needed to silence the sceptics seems debatable.

10

Cloning Benefits Animals

Robert P. Lanza, Betsy L. Dresser, and Philip Damiani

Robert P. Lanza is vice president of medical and scientific development at Advanced Cell Technology (ACT) and founder of the South Meadow Pond and Wildlife Association in Worcester, Massachusetts. Betsy L. Dresser is senior vice president for research at the Audubon Institute as well as director of both the Audubon Institute Center for Research of Endangered Species and the Freeport-McMoRan Audubon Species Survival Center. Philip Damiani, a research scientist at ACT, is a member of the International Embryo Transfer Society's committee on cryopreservation.

Cloning, a process whereby scientists duplicate an animal by copying its cells and implanting them into another animal for gestation, benefits wildlife. For species with few existing individuals left, scientists can clone animals that have died, sending new genes back into the gene pool to maintain and even increase genetic diversity. The remaining endangered animals are free from the stress of implantation and surrogate motherhood, since an animal of a different species carries and gives birth to the clone. More importantly, extinct species may one day be reincarnated by cloning tissue that has been preserved in ice.

In late November [2000] a humble Iowa cow is slated to give birth to the world's first cloned endangered species, a baby bull to be named Noah. Noah is a gaur: a member of a species of large oxlike animals that are now rare in their homelands of India, Indochina and southeast Asia. These one-ton bovines have been hunted for sport for generations. More recently the gaur's habitats of forests, bamboo jungles and grasslands have dwindled to the point that only roughly 36,000 are thought to remain in the wild. The World Conservation Union–IUCN [International Union for Conservation of Nature and Natural Resources] Red Data Book [of threatened species] lists the gaur as endangered, and trade in live gaur or gaur products—whether horns, hides or hooves—is banned by the Convention on International Trade in Endangered Species (CITES).

But if all goes as predicted, in a few weeks a spindly-legged little Noah will trot in a new day in the conservation of his kind as well as in the preservation of many other endangered species. Perhaps most important, he will be living, mooing proof that one animal can carry and give birth to the exact genetic duplicate, or clone, of an animal of a different species. And Noah will be just the first creature up the ramp of the ark of endangered species that we and other scientists are currently attempting to clone: plans are under way to clone the African bongo antelope, the Sumatran tiger and that favorite of zoo lovers, the reluctant-to-reproduce giant panda. Cloning could also reincarnate some species that are already extinct—most immediately, perhaps, the bucardo mountain goat of Spain. The last bucardo—a female—died of a smashed skull when a tree fell on it early [in 2000], but Spanish scientists have preserved some of its cells.

Cloning [offers] a way to preserve and propagate endangered species that reproduce poorly in zoos until their habitats can be restored and they can be reintroduced to the wild.

Advances in cloning offer a way to preserve and propagate endangered species that reproduce poorly in zoos until their habitats can be restored and they can be reintroduced to the wild. Cloning's main power, however, is that it allows researchers to introduce new genes back into the gene pool of a species that has few remaining animals. Most zoos are not equipped to collect and cryopreserve semen; similarly, eggs are difficult to obtain and are damaged by freezing. But by cloning animals whose body cells have been preserved, scientists can keep the genes of that individual alive, maintaining (and in some instances increasing) the overall genetic diversity of endangered populations of that species.

Nevertheless, some conservation biologists have been slow to recognize the benefits of basic assisted reproduction strategies, such as in vitro fertilization, and have been hesitant to consider cloning. Although we agree that every effort should be made to preserve wild spaces for the incredible diversity of life that inhabits this planet, in some cases either the battle has already been lost or its outcome looks dire. Cloning technology is not a panacea, but it offers the opportunity to save some of the species that contribute to that diversity. A clone still requires a mother, however, and very few conservationists would advocate rounding up wild female endangered animals for that purpose or subjecting a precious zoo resident of the same species to the rigors of assisted reproduction and surrogate motherhood. That means that to clone an endangered species, researchers such as ourselves must solve the problem of how to get cells from two different species to yield the clone of one. . . .

Initial successes

We expect that the first few endangered species to be cloned will be those whose reproduction has already been well studied. Several zoos and conservation societies—including the Audubon Institute Center for Research of Endangered Species (AICRES) in New Orleans, which is led by one of us (Dresser)—have probed the reproductive biology of a range of endangered species. with some notable successes. [In November 1999], for example, Dresser and her colleagues reported the first transplantation of a previously frozen embryo of an endangered animal into another species that resulted in a live birth. In this case, an ordinary house cat gave birth to an African wildcat, a species that has declined in some areas.

So far, beyond the African wildcat and the gaur, we and others have accomplished interspecies embryo transfers in four additional cases: an Indian desert cat into a domestic cat; a bongo antelope into a more common African antelope called an eland; a mouflon sheep into a domestic sheep; and a rare red deer into a common white-tailed deer. All yielded live births. We hope that the studies of felines will pave the way for cloning the cheetah, of which only roughly 12,000 remain in southern Africa. The prolonged courtship behavior of cheetahs requires substantial territory, a possible explanation for why the animals have bred so poorly in zoos and yet another reason to fear their extinction as their habitat shrinks.

Potential cloning of pandas

One of the most exciting candidates for endangered-species cloning—the giant panda—has not yet been the subject of interspecies transfer experiments, but it has benefited from assisted reproduction technology. Following the well-publicized erotic fumblings of the National Zoo's ill-fated panda pair, the late Ling-Ling and Hsing-Hsing, the San Diego Zoo turned to artificial insemination to make proud parents of its Bai Yun and Shi Shi. Baby Hua Mei was born in August 1999.

Giant pandas are such emblems of endangered species that the World Wildlife Fund (WWF) uses one in its logo. According to a census that is now almost 20 years old, fewer than 1,000 pandas remain in their mountainous habitats of bamboo forest in southwest China. But some biologists think that the population might have rebounded a bit in some areas. The WWF [is conducting] a census of China's pandas to produce a better estimate.

In the meantime, we at ACT [Advanced Cell Technology] are discussing plans with the government of China to clone a giant panda. Chinese scientists have already made strides toward the goal of panda cloning. In August 1999 Chen Dayuan of the institute and his co-workers published a paper in the English-language journal *Science* in China announcing that they had fused panda skeletal muscle, uterus and mammary gland cells with the eggs of a rabbit and then coaxed the cloned cells to develop into blastocysts [cells that can be implanted for gestation] in the laboratory.

Cloning endangered species is controversial, but we assert that it has an important place in plans to manage species that are in danger of extinction.

A rabbit, of course, is too small to serve as a surrogate mother for a giant panda. Instead ACT and the Chinese plan to turn to American black bears. As this issue of *Scientific American* goes to press [in 2000], ACT is finalizing plans to obtain eggs from female black bears killed during this autumn's hunting season in the northeastern U.S. Together with the Chinese,

ACT scientists hope to use these eggs and frozen cells from the late Hsing-Hsing or Ling-Ling to generate cloned giant panda embryos that can be implanted into a female black bear now living in a zoo. A research group that includes veterinarians at Bear Country U.S.A. in Rapid City, S.D., has already demonstrated that black bears can give birth to transplanted embryos. They reported the successful birth of a black bear cub from an embryo transferred from one pregnant black bear to another last year in the journal *Theriogenology*. [By mid-2004, no panda had been successfully cloned.]

AICRES scientists hope to take advantage of the success with bongo antelope that one of us (Dresser) had while at the Cincinnati Zoo. In 1984 Dresser and Charles Earle Pope of the University of Alabama at Birmingham (now with AICRES and Louisiana State University) and their colleagues announced the birth of a bongo after moving very early embryos from a pregnant female bongo to an eland surrogate mother.

Most of the mountain subspecies of bongo—a medium-size antelope with vertical white stripes—live in captivity. According to the World Conservation Union–IUCN, the mountain bongo is endangered, with only 50 or so remaining in a small region of Kenya. In contrast, the 1999 Bongo International Studbook lists nearly 550 mountain bongo living in zoos throughout the world. The lowland bongo subspecies is slightly better off: it is listed as "near threatened" and has a population of perhaps several thousand scattered throughout central and western Africa.

A coalition of conservation organizations in the U.S. and Kenya is now planning to send mountain bongo that have been bred in captivity to two sites in Kenya. And in a new approach to reintroducing a species, AICRES is working in Kenya to transfer frozen bongo embryos into eland surrogates. Cloning could support these efforts and possibly yield more bongo for reintroduction.

Resurrection of extinct species

But what about animals that are already extinct? Chances are slim to nil that scientists will soon be able to clone dinosaurs, à la Jurassic Park, or woolly mammoths. The primary problem is the dearth of preserved tissue—and hence DNA. A group of researchers unearthed what they had hoped would be a well-preserved mammoth [in 1999], but repeated freezing and thawing over the eons had poked holes in the creature's DNA, and molecular biologists have not yet found a feasible way of filling in such genetic gaps.

A similar difficulty has hobbled efforts by Australian scientists to clone a thylacine, or Tasmanian tiger, a wolflike marsupial that died out in the 1930s. Researchers at the Australian Museum in Sydney are attempting to clone cells from a thylacine pup that was preserved in alcohol in 1866, but the DNA is in such poor condition that they say they will have to reconstruct all of the animal's chromosomes.

The recently extinct bucardo may prove a more promising target for resurrection. ACT is arranging a collaboration with Alberto Fernández-Arias and José Folch of the Agricultural Research Service in Zaragoza, Spain. Fernández-Arias froze tissue from the last bucardo. He and Folch had tried for several years to preserve the mountain goat, which in the end was wiped out by poaching, habitat destruction and landslides. Last year they transferred embryos from a subspecies related to the bucardo to a domestic goat, yielding live kids.

While habitat preservation is the keystone of species conservation, some countries are too poor or too unstable to support sustainable conservation efforts.

But even if interspecies nuclear transfer [a technique used in cloning] succeeds for the bucardo, it will yield only a sorority of clones, because we have tissue from just one animal, a female. ACT plans to try to make a male by removing one copy of the X chromosome from one of the female bucardo's cells and using a tiny artificial cell called a microsome to add a Y chromosome from a closely related goat species. The technology has been used by other researchers to manipulate human chromosomes, but it has never before been used for cloning. A nonprofit organization called the Soma Foundation has been established to help fund such efforts.

Why clone?

Cloning endangered species is controversial, but we assert that it has an important place in plans to manage species that are in danger of extinction. Some researchers have argued against it, maintaining that it would restrict an already dwindling amount of genetic diversity for those species. Not so. We advocate the establishment of a worldwide network of repositories to hold frozen tissue from all the individuals of an endangered species from which it is possible to collect samples. Those cells—like the sperm and eggs now being collected in "frozen zoos" by a variety of zoological parks—could serve as a genetic trust for reconstituting entire populations of a given species. Such an enterprise would be relatively inexpensive: a typical three-foot freezer can hold more than 2,000 samples and uses just a few dollars of electricity per year. [As of 2000] only AICRES and the San Diego Zoo's Center for Reproduction of Endangered Species maintained banks of frozen body cells that could be used for cloning.

Other critics claim that the practice could overshadow efforts to preserve habitat. We counter that while habitat preservation is the keystone of species conservation, some countries are too poor or too unstable to support sustainable conservation efforts. What is more, the continued growth of the human species will probably make it impossible to save enough habitat for some other species. Cloning by interspecies nuclear transfer offers the possibility of keeping the genetic stock of those species on hand without maintaining populations in captivity, which is a particularly costly enterprise in the case of large animals.

Another argument against cloning endangered species is that it might siphon donor money away from habitat maintenance. But not all potential donors are willing to support efforts to stem the tide of habitat destruction. We should recognize that some who would otherwise not donate to preserve endangered species at all might want to support cloning or other assisted reproduction technologies.

The time to act is now.

11

Modern Slaughtering Methods Are Humane

American Meat Institute

Founded in Chicago in 1906, the American Meat Institute is a membership trade organization that represents the interests of the meat and poultry industries. It researches and educates in areas such as animal welfare and food safety.

Livestock welfare has improved continuously since 1998 as a result of animal scientist Temple Grandin's pioneering research, which examined ways to improve conditions for animals. As one of the most heavily regulated industries in the nation, the meat industry has safeguarded the welfare of its animals through mandatory inspections and voluntary self-audits to ensure humane animal handling, stunning, and slaughter.

Treating livestock in packing plants humanely is ethically appropriate. It has many other benefits as well, including:
- More efficient plants
- Safer workplaces
- Better attitudes among employees
- Improved meat quality

During the 1990s, the academic community placed more emphasis on animal behavior. As they did, the "science" of livestock welfare evolved. And as it evolved, so too did the meat packing industry's attitude toward livestock and its understanding of the value of animal handling, training, and auditing programs.

A survey of AMI [American Meat Institute] members in 2001 showed that more than 93 percent of beef and 92 percent of pork plants routinely conduct animal handling self-audits. In addition, meat plants that supply to major retail and foodservice chains are audited routinely as a condition of business.

The emphasis on animal handling has resulted in positive changes that are best reflected in continuous, documented improvements in animal welfare in packing plants [since 1998].

Government oversight

The U.S. meat industry is one of the most heavily regulated industries in the nation. Thousands of pages of regulations govern every aspect of the meat packing business, including how livestock are treated. The Humane Slaughter Act of 1978 dictates strict animal handling and slaughtering practices for packing plants. Those standards are monitored by Food Safety and Inspection Service (FSIS) inspectors nationwide, who are present in packing plants during every minute of operation. FSIS inspectors are empowered to take action in a plant any time they identify a violation of the Act. Key requirements under the Act specify:

- That animals must be handled and moved through chutes and pens in ways that do not cause stress.
- That livestock must be rendered insensible to pain prior to slaughter. The Act details the methods that must be used to stun animals.
- That animals must have access to water and that those kept longer than 24 hours have access to feed.
- That animals kept in pens overnight must be permitted plenty of room to lie down.
- That "downed" or crippled livestock in the stockyards, crowd pens or stunning chutes may not be dragged.

In 2002, USDA [U.S. Department of Agriculture] added 17 new District Veterinary Medical Officers to the FSIS team. These DVMOs are focusing their efforts on animal handling in plants and perform regular audits of handling and stunning practices.

The science of livestock welfare

What was once thought of as a regulatory requirement and an ethical obligation today has become a literal science. Throughout the 1990s, research in the area of animal handling, stunning and stress shed new light on ways to improve conditions for animals. Temple Grandin, Ph.D., of Colorado State University has been one of the leading researchers in this area.

Grandin's pioneering work has helped the meat industry understand how to design plants in ways that encourage livestock to move forward without being prodded, how to drive animals without the use of stressful electric prods, how to ensure that floors prevent slippages that can cause injuries and how to minimize distractions that can cause animals to balk and force employees to prod them.

Better regulations

In the early 1990s, Grandin helped the industry take humane slaughter regulations a step further through the development of *Recommended Animal Handling Guidelines for Meat Packers.*

These guidelines provided detailed illustrations depicting how to ensure optimal handling and stunning in packing plants. Since that time, Grandin has helped the meat industry develop numerous other educational tools as well. . . .

In addition to her academic efforts, Grandin has been retained by the U.S. government and by foreign governments to conduct audits of packing plants to assess handling and stunning practices. As a result of these efforts, Grandin concluded that there are means of objectively "scoring" and evaluating animal handling and stunning. She in turn recommended that plants conduct regular self-audits to assess handling and stunning in plants.

The AMI Foundation has incorporated audits into a set of *Good Management Practices for Animal Handling and Stunning*—practices it encourages all plants to follow. As a result, self-audits are now conducted routinely by the industry. In fact, a 2001 survey of AMI members showed that more than 90 percent of respondents now conduct self-audits.

Handling and stunning improvements

Data collected by Grandin through surveys done in 1996, 1999, 2000, 2001 and 2002 have demonstrated consistent, sustained improvement in livestock handling and stunning (http://www.grandin.com).

In addition, a 2001 survey of American Meat Institute members reflects an increasing focus on animal handling and stunning by meat plants. According to the results, 93 percent of beef plants and 92 percent of pork plants conduct animal handling and stunning self-audits. Twenty-three percent of auditing beef plants and 32 percent of auditing pork plants said their audits had resulted in strong improvements in handling/stunning. Seventy percent of auditing beef plants and 73 percent of auditing pork plants report modest improvements in animal handling and stunning.

Seventy-nine percent of beef plants and 81 percent of pork plants indicated that they had hired a consultant to resolve animal handling and stunning problems. Ninety-three percent of beef plants and 81 percent of pork plants said they had purchased special equipment like a restrainer to improve handling and/or stunning.

A report to Congress by the Food Safety and Inspection Service (FSIS) in March 2003 indicated that virtually all of the infractions documented by FSIS inspectors in 2002 were related to facility problems like slippery floors or large gaps between pen bars.

Still, the U.S. meat industry is committed to finding new ways to enhance animal handling and stunning in plants even further.

12

Modern Slaughtering Methods Are Inhumane

Joby Warrick

Joby Warrick is an investigative staff writer for the Washington Post.

Although the Humane Slaughter Act dictates that farm animals must be stunned before they are killed to minimize pain, it has been documented that, due to improper stunning and handling, some farm animals are butchered alive, piece by piece. Due to relaxed oversight and enforcement of the Humane Slaughter Act, these violations often go unpunished. Making matters worse, the U.S. Department of Agriculture no longer tracks violations of the Humane Slaughter Act, enabling slaughtering plants to continue to harm animals.

It takes 25 minutes to turn a live steer into steak at the modern slaughterhouse where Ramon Moreno works. For 20 years, his post was "second-legger," a job that entails cutting hocks off carcasses as they whirl past at a rate of 309 an hour.

The cattle were supposed to be dead before they got to Moreno. But too often they weren't.

"They blink. They make noises," he says softly. "The head moves, the eyes are wide and looking around."

Still Moreno would cut. On bad days, he says, dozens of animals reached his station clearly alive and conscious. Some would survive as far as the tail cutter, the belly ripper, the hide puller. "They die," says Moreno, "piece by piece."

Under a 23-year-old federal law, slaughtered cattle and hogs first must be "stunned"—rendered insensible to pain—with a blow to the head or an electric shock. But at overtaxed plants, the law is sometimes broken, with cruel consequences for animals as well as workers. Enforcement records, interviews, videos and worker affidavits describe repeated violations of the Humane Slaughter Act at dozens of slaughterhouses, ranging from the smallest, custom butcheries to modern, automated establishments such as the sprawling IBP Inc. plant here where Moreno works.

"In plants all over the United States, this happens on a daily basis," says Lester Friedlander, a veterinarian and formerly chief government inspector at a Pennsylvania hamburger plant. "I've seen it happen. And I've talked to other veterinarians. They feel it's out of control."

Violations go unpunished

The U.S. Department of Agriculture [USDA] oversees the treatment of animals in meat plants, but enforcement of the law varies dramatically. While a few plants have been forced to halt production for a few hours because of alleged animal cruelty, such sanctions are rare.

For example, the government took no action against a Texas beef company that was cited 22 times in 1998 for violations that included chopping hooves off live cattle. In another case, agency supervisors failed to take action on multiple complaints of animal cruelty at a Florida beef plant and fired an animal health technician for reporting the problems to the Humane Society. The dismissal letter sent to the technician, Tim Walker, said his disclosure had "irreparably damaged" the agency's relations with the packing plant.

"I complained to everyone—I said, 'Lookit, they're skinning live cows in there,'"Walker says. "Always it was the same answer: 'We know it's true. But there's nothing we can do about it.'"

In the past three years, a new meat inspection system that shifted responsibility to industry has made it harder to catch and report cruelty problems, some federal inspectors say. Under the new system, implemented in 1998, the agency no longer tracks the number of humane-slaughter violations its inspectors find each year.

Some inspectors are so frustrated they're asking outsiders for help: The inspectors' union last spring [2000] urged Washington state authorities to crack down on alleged animal abuse at the IBP plant in Pasco. In a statement, IBP said problems described by workers in its Washington state plant "do not accurately represent the way we operate our plants. We take the issue of proper livestock handling very seriously."

But the union complained that new government policies and faster production speeds at the plant had "significantly hampered our ability to ensure compliance." Several animal welfare groups joined in the petition.

"Privatization of meat inspection has meant a quiet death to the already meager enforcement of the Humane Slaughter Act," says Gail Eisnitz of the Humane Farming Association, a group that advocates better treatment of farm animals. "USDA isn't simply relinquishing its humane-slaughter oversight to the meat industry, but is—without the knowledge and consent of Congress—abandoning this function altogether."

The meat industry's response

The USDA's Food Safety Inspection Service, which is responsible for meat inspection, says it has not relaxed its oversight. In January, the agency ordered a review of 100 slaughterhouses. An FSIS [Food Safety and Inspection Service] memo reminded its 7,600 inspectors they had an "obligation to ensure compliance" with humane-handling laws.

The review comes as pressure grows on both industry and regulators to improve conditions for the 155 million cattle, hogs, horses and sheep slaughtered each year. McDonald's and Burger King have been subject to boycotts by animal rights groups protesting mistreatment of livestock.

As a result, two years ago McDonald's began requiring suppliers to abide by the American Meat Institute's Good Management Practices for Animal Handling and Stunning. The company also began conducting annual audits of meat plants. Two weeks ago [April 2001], Burger King announced it would require suppliers to follow the meat institute's standards.

"Burger King Corp. takes the issues of food safety and animal welfare very seriously, and we expect our suppliers to comply," the company said in a statement.

Some would survive as far as the tail cutter, the belly ripper, the hide puller.

Industry groups acknowledge that sloppy killing has tangible consequences for consumers as well as company profits. Fear and pain cause animals to produce hormones that damage meat and cost companies tens of millions of dollars a year in discarded product, according to industry estimates. Industry officials say they also recognize an ethical imperative to treat animals with compassion. Science is blurring the distinction between the mental processes of humans and lower animals—discovering, for example, that even the lowly rat may dream. Americans thus are becoming more sensitive to the suffering of food animals, even as they consume increasing numbers of them.

"Handling animals humanely," says American Meat Institute President J. Patrick Boyle, "is just right thing to do."

Clearly, not all plants have gotten the message.

Evidence of inhumane practices

A *Washington Post* computer analysis of government enforcement records found 527 violations of humane-handling regulations from 1996 to 1997, the last years for which complete records were available. The offenses range from overcrowded stockyards to incidents in which live animals were cut, skinned or scalded.

Through the Freedom of Information Act, *The Post* obtained enforcement documents from 28 plants that had high numbers of offenses or had drawn penalties for violating humane-handling laws. *The Post* also interviewed dozens of current and former federal meat inspectors and slaughterhouse workers. A reporter reviewed affidavits and secret video recordings made inside two plants.

Among the findings:

• One Texas plant, Supreme Beef Packers in Ladonia, had 22 violations in six months. During one inspection, federal officials found nine live cattle dangling from an overhead chain. But managers at the plant, which announced last fall it was ceasing operations, resisted USDA warnings, saying its practices were no different than others in the industry. "Other plants are not subject to such extensive scrutiny of their stunning over activities," the plant complained in a 1997 letter to the USDA.

• Government inspectors halted production for a day at the Calhoun Packing Co. beef plant in Palestine, Tex., after inspectors saw cattle being improperly stunned. "They were still conscious and had good reflexes," B.V. Swamy, a veterinarian and senior USDA official at the plant, wrote. The shift supervisor "allowed the cattle to be hung anyway." IBP, which owned the plant at the time, contested the findings but "took steps to resolve the situation," including installing video equipment and increasing training, a spokesman said. IBP has since sold the plant.

• At the Farmers Livestock Cooperative processing plant in Hawaii, inspectors documented 14 humane-slaughter violations in as many months. Records from 1997 and 1998 describe hogs that were walking and squealing after being stunned as many as four times. In a memo to USDA, the company said it fired the stunner and increased monitoring of the slaughter process.

• At an Excel Corp. beef plant in Fort Morgan, Colo., production was halted for a day in 1998 after workers allegedly cut off the leg of a live cow whose limbs had become wedged in a piece of machinery. In imposing the sanction, U.S. inspectors cited a string of violations in the previous two years, including the cutting and skinning of live cattle. The company, responding to one such charge, contended that it was normal for animals to blink and arch their backs after being stunned, and such "muscular reaction" can occur up to six hours after death. "None of these reactions indicate the animal is still alive," the company wrote to USDA.

• Hogs, unlike cattle, are dunked in tanks of hot water after they are stunned to soften the hides for skinning. As a result, a botched slaughter condemns some hogs to being scalded and drowned. Secret videotape from an Iowa pork plant shows hogs squealing and kicking as they are being lowered into the water.

Grandin's audits

USDA documents and interviews with inspectors and plant workers attributed many of the problems to poor training, faulty or poorly maintained equipment or excessive production speeds. Those problems were identified five years ago in an industry-wide audit by Temple Grandin, an assistant professor with Colorado State University's animal sciences department and one of the nation's leading experts on slaughter practices.

"USDA isn't simply relinquishing its humane-slaughter oversight to the meat industry, but is— without the knowledge and consent of Congress—abandoning this function altogether."

In the early 1990s, Grandin developed the first objective standards for treatment of animals in slaughterhouses, which were adopted by the American Meat Institute, the industry's largest trade group. Her initial, USDA-funded survey in 1996 was one of the first attempts to grade slaughter plants.

One finding was a high failure rate among beef plants that use stunning devices known as "captive-bolt" guns. Of the plants surveyed, only 36 percent earned a rating of "acceptable" or better, meaning cattle were knocked unconscious with a single blow at least 95 percent of the time.

Grandin now conducts annual surveys as a consultant for the American Meat Institute and McDonald's Corp. She maintains that the past four years have brought dramatic improvements—mostly because of pressure from McDonald's, which sends a team of meat industry auditors into dozens of plants each year to observe slaughter practices.

Workers allegedly cut off the leg of a live cow whose limbs had become wedged in a piece of machinery.

Based on the data collected by McDonald's auditors, the portion of beef plants scoring "acceptable" or better climbed to 90 percent in 1999. Some workers and inspectors are skeptical of the McDonald's numbers, and Grandin says the industry's performance dropped slightly last year after auditors stopped giving notice of some inspections.

Grandin says high production speeds can trigger problems when people and equipment are pushed beyond their capacity. From a typical kill rate of 50 cattle an hour in the early 1900s, production speeds rose dramatically in the 1980s. They now approach 400 per hour in the newest plants.

"It's like the 'I Love Lucy' episode in the chocolate factory," she says. "You can speed up a job and speed up a job, and after a while you get to a point where performance doesn't simply decline—it crashes."

When that happens, it's not only animals that suffer. Industry trade groups acknowledge that improperly stunned animals contribute to worker injuries in an industry that already has the nation's highest rate of job-related injuries and illnesses—about 27 percent a year. At some plants, "dead" animals have inflicted so many broken limbs and teeth that workers wear chest pads and hockey masks.

"The live cows cause a lot of injuries," says Martin Fuentes, an IBP worker whose arm was kicked and shattered by a dying cow. "The line is never stopped simply because an animal is alive."

Improper stunning

At IBP's Pasco complex, the making of the American hamburger starts in a noisy, blood-spattered chamber shielded from view by a stainless steel wall. Here, live cattle emerge from a narrow chute to be dispatched in a process known as "knocking" or "stunning." On most days the chamber is manned by a pair of Mexican immigrants who speak little English and earn about $9 an hour for killing up to 2,050 head per shift.

The tool of choice is the captive-bolt gun, which fires a retractable metal rod into the steer's forehead. An effective stunning requires a precision shot, which workers must deliver hundreds of times daily to balky, frightened animals that frequently weigh 1,000 pounds or more. Within 12 seconds of entering the chamber, the fallen steer is shackled to a moving chain to be bled and butchered by other workers in a fast-moving production line.

The hitch, IBP workers say, is that some "stunned" cattle wake up.

"If you put a knife into the cow, it's going to make a noise: It says, 'Moo!'" says Moreno, the former second-legger, who began working in the stockyard last year. "They move the head and the eyes and the leg like the cow wants to walk."

After a blow to the head, an unconscious animal may kick or twitch by reflex. But a videotape, made secretly by IBP workers and reviewed by veterinarians for *The Post*, depicts cattle that clearly are alive and conscious after being stunned.

Some cattle, dangling by a leg from the plant's overhead chain, twist and arch their backs as though trying to right themselves. Close-ups show blinking reflexes, an unmistakable sign of a conscious brain, according to guidelines approved by the American Meat Institute.

The video, parts of which were aired by Seattle television station KING last spring, shows injured cattle being trampled. In one graphic scene, workers give a steer electric shocks by jamming a battery-powered prod into its mouth.

More than 20 workers signed affidavits alleging that the violations shown on tape are commonplace and that supervisors are aware of them. The sworn statements and videos were prepared with help from the Humane Farming Association. Some workers had taken part in a 1999 strike over what they said were excessive plant production speeds.

Slaughtered alive

"I've seen thousands and thousands of cows go through the slaughter process alive," IBP veteran Fuentes, the worker who was injured while working on live cattle, said in an affidavit. "The cows can get seven minutes down the line and still be alive. I've been in the side-puller where they're still alive. All the hide is stripped out down the neck there."

IBP, the nation's top beef processor, denounced as an "appalling aberration" the problems captured on the tape. It suggested the events may have been staged by "activists trying to raise money and promote their agenda. . . .

In one graphic scene, workers give a steer electric shocks by jamming a battery-powered prod into its mouth.

"Like many other people, we were very upset over the hidden camera video," the company said. "We do not in any way condone some of the livestock handling that was shown."

After the video surfaced, IBP increased worker training and installed cameras in the slaughter area. The company also questioned workers and offered a reward for information leading to identification of those responsible for the video. One worker said IBP pressured him to sign a statement denying that he had seen live cattle on the line.

"I knew that what I wrote wasn't true," says the worker, who did not want to be identified for fear of losing his job. "Cows still go alive every day. When cows go alive, it's because they don't give me time to kill them."

Independent assessments of the workers' claims have been inconclusive. Washington state officials launched a probe in May that included an unannounced plant inspection. The investigators say they were detained outside the facility for an hour while their identities were checked. They saw no acts of animal cruelty once permitted inside.

Grandin, the Colorado State professor, also inspected IBP's plant, at the company's request; that inspection was announced. Although she observed no live cattle being butchered, she concluded that the plant's older-style equipment was "overloaded." Grandin reviewed parts of the workers' videotape and said there was no mistaking what she saw.

"There were fully alive beef on that rail," Grandin says.

Obstacles

Preventing this kind of suffering is officially a top priority for the USDA's Food Safety Inspection Service. By law, a humane-slaughter violation is among a handful of offenses that can result in an immediate halt in production—and cost a meatpacker hundreds or even thousands of dollars per idle minute. In reality, many inspectors describe humane slaughter as a blind spot: Inspectors' regular duties rarely take them to the chambers where stunning occurs. Inconsistencies in enforcement, training and record-keeping hamper the agency's ability to identify problems.

The meat inspectors' union, in its petition last spring to Washington state's attorney general, contended that federal agents are "often prevented from carrying out" the mandate against animal cruelty. Among the obstacles inspectors face are "dramatic increases in production speeds, lack of support from supervisors in plants and district offices . . . new inspection policies which significantly reduce our enforcement authority, and little to no access to the areas of the plants where animals are killed," stated the petition by the National Joint Council of Food Inspection Locals.

Barbara Masters, the agency's director of slaughter operations, told meat industry executives in February she didn't know if the number of violations was up or down, though she believed most plants were complying with the law. "We encourage the district offices to monitor trends," she said. "The fact that we haven't heard anything suggests there are no trends."

But some inspectors see little evidence the agency is interested in hearing about problems. Under the new inspection system, the USDA stopped tracking the number of violations and dropped all mentions of humane slaughter from its list of rotating tasks for inspectors.

The agency says it expects its watchdogs to enforce the law anyway. Many inspectors still do, though some occasionally wonder if it's worth the trouble.

"It always ends up in argument: Instead of re-stunning the animal, you spend 20 minutes just talking about it," says Colorado meat inspector Gary Dahl, sharing his private views. "Yes, the animal will be dead in a few minutes anyway. But why not let him die with dignity?"

Organizations to Contact

The editors have compiled the following list of organizations concerned with the issues debated in this book. The descriptions are derived from materials provided by the organizations. All have publications or information available for interested readers. The list was compiled on the date of publication of the present volume; the information provided here may change. Be aware that many organizations take several weeks or longer to respond to inquiries, so allow as much time as possible.

Advanced Cell Technology (ACT)
One Innovation Dr., Biotech Three, Worcester, MA 01605
(508) 756-1212 • fax: (508) 756-4468
Web site: www.advancedcell.com

The first to successfully clone an endangered animal by duplicating its cells and implanting them into another species, ACT also engages in animal cloning for technology development and drug screening. Its Web site contains links to reports and press releases that are published in various scientific magazines, as well as to testimonial, letters, and reports regarding the ethical issues of cloning.

American Anti-Vivisection Society (AAVS)
801 Old York Rd., Suite 204, Jenkintown, PA 19046-1685
(215) 887-0816 • fax: (215) 887-2088
e-mail: aavs@aavs.org • Web site: www.aavs.org

AAVS advocates the abolition of vivisection, opposes all types of experiments on living animals, and sponsors research on alternatives to these methods. The society produces videos and publishes numerous brochures as well as the award-winning *AV Magazine*, whose issues are each dedicated to a different topic concerning animals, such as vivisection in education and animal testing alternatives.

American Meat Institute (AMI)
1700 North Moore St., Suite 1600, Arlington, VA 22209
(703) 841-2400 • fax: (703) 527-0938
Web site: www.meatami.com

Founded in 1906, AMI is a membership trade organization that represents the interests of the meat and poultry industries. It researches and educates in areas such as animal welfare and food safety. The AMI Web site posts news releases, fact sheets, info kits, and visual aids relating to animal care.

American Society for the Prevention of Cruelty to Animals (ASPCA)
424 East 92nd St., New York, NY 10128-6804
(212) 876-7700 • fax: (212) 348-3031
e-mail: press@aspca.org • Web site: www.aspca.org

The ASPCA promotes appreciation for and humane treatment of animals, encourages enforcement of anticruelty laws, and works for the passage of legislation that strengthens existing animal protection laws. In addition to making available books, brochures, and videos on animal issues, the ASPCA publishes *Animal Watch*, a quarterly magazine.

Animal Legal Defense Fund (ALDF)
127 Fourth St., Petaluma, CA 94952-3005
(707) 769-7771 • fax: (707) 769-0785
e-mail: info@aldf.org • Web site: www.aldf.org

ALDF is an organization of attorneys and law students who promote animal rights and protect the lives and interests of animals through the use of their legal skills. It publishes the *Animals' Advocate* quarterly.

AnimalScam
The Center for Consumer Freedom
PO Box 27414, Washington, DC 20038
Web site: www.animalscam.com

AnimalScam is a project of the Center for Consumer Freedom, a nonprofit organization that promotes personal responsibility and protects consumers' choices. AnimalScam refutes claims made by animal rights activists, reveals what it says are hidden agendas of animal rights groups, and protects the rights of Americans to eat meat, drink milk, wear fur, and visit zoos. News articles, quotes by animal rights activists, and anti-animal-rights-groups ads are posted on its Web site.

Farm Animal Reform Movement (FARM)
PO Box 30654, Bethesda, MD 20824
(888) ASK-FARM
e-mail: farm@farmusa.org • Web site: www.farmusa.org

FARM seeks to moderate and eliminate animal suffering and other adverse impacts of commercial animal production. It promotes the annual observance of March 20 as the "Great American Meatout," a day of meatless meals, and provides a variety of brochures and fact sheets for consumers and activists.

Foundation for Biomedical Research (FBR)
818 Connecticut Ave. NW, Suite 303, Washington, DC 20006
(202) 457-0654 • fax: (202) 457-0659
Web site: www.fbresearch.org

FBR provides information and educational programs about what it sees as the necessary and important role of laboratory animals in biomedical research and testing. Its videos include *Waiting for a Cure* and *Caring for Life*. It also publishes a newsletter, *Foundation for Biomedical Research*.

Fund for Animals
200 West 57th St., New York, NY 10019
(888) 405-FUND • (212) 246-2096 • fax: (212) 246-2633
e-mail: fundinfo@fund.org • Web site: www.fund.org

The Fund for Animals encourages children and adults to deal with animals more humanely. It publicizes animal protection issues, facilitates the passage of proanimal legislation, and helps to stave off bills that allow animals to be exploited or harmed. Numerous fact sheets, press releases, and reports are available on its Web site, as is a link to free subscriptions of its quarterly newspaper for teens, *Animal Free Press*.

Great Ape Project (GAP)
PO Box 19492, Portland, OR 97280-0492
(503) 222-5755 • fax: (503) 238-5884
Web site: www.greatapeproject.org

GAP, an international organization, works to include great apes within the category of persons. It advocates that due to their humanlike mental capacities and emotions, great apes deserve the same basic moral and legal rights as people enjoy. GAP publishes a free newsletter called *GAPNews;* its books include *The Great Ape Project: Equality Beyond Humanity* and *The Great Ape Project Census.*

Humane Society of the United States (HSUS)
2100 L St. NW, Washington, DC 20037
(202) 452-1100 • fax: (202) 778-6132
Web site: www.hsus.org

HSUS works to foster respect, understanding, and compassion for all creatures. Among its many diverse efforts, it maintains programs supporting responsible pet ownership and the elimination of cruelty in hunting and trapping. It also exposes painful uses of animals in research and testing and abusive treatment of animals in movies, circuses, pulling contests, and racing. It campaigns for animal protection legislation and monitors the enforcement of existing animal protection statutes. HSUS publishes the quarterlies *All Animals* and *HSUS News.*

Institute for Animal Rights Law
6 Overlook Rd., Santa Fe, NM 87505
fax: (505) 989-3300
Web site: www.instituteforanimalrightslaw.org

The Institute for Animal Rights Law provides legal information, analysis, and guidance for the animal rights and animal welfare movements. Among other accomplishments, it has drafted state and federal animal protection legislation, advises public officials and animal rights groups about the legal rights of animals, and educates the public about animal rights issues. Its Web site offers model statutes, federal animal protection statutes, and articles pertaining to animal rights law.

Institute of Laboratory Animal Research (ILAR)
2101 Constitution Ave. NW, Washington, DC 20418
(202) 334-2590
Web site: http://dels.nas.edu

Organized under the auspices of the National Academy of Sciences, ILAR advises, upon request, the federal government and other agencies concerning the use of animals in biomedical research. It prepares guidelines and policy papers on biotechnology, the use of animals in precollege education, and other topics in laboratory animal science. Its publications include *Guide for the Care and Use of Laboratory Animals* and the quarterly *ILAR News.*

The Jane Goodall Institute for Wildlife Research, Education, and Conservation (JGI)
8700 Georgia Ave., Suite 500, Silver Spring, MD 20910-3605
(301) 565-0086 • fax: (301) 565-3188
Web site: www.janegoodall.org

JGI's goals include the support and expansion of field research on wild chimpanzees, assisting studies of chimps in captive environments, conducting comparative studies of captive and free-living chimpanzees, and enriching captive chimpanzees' lives. JGI also participates in conservation programs in Africa. It publishes the semiannual *Roots & Shoots Network* newsletter for members.

Johns Hopkins Center for Alternatives to Animal Testing (CAAT)
111 Market Pl., Suite 840, Baltimore, MD 21202-6709
(410) 223-1693 • fax: (410) 223-1603
e-mail: caat@jhsph.edu • Web site: http://caat.jhsph.edu

CAAT fosters the development of scientifically acceptable alternatives to animal testing for use in creating and evaluating the safety of commercial and therapeutic products. The center conducts symposia for researchers and corporations. One of its publications is *Animals and Alternatives in Testing: History, Science, and Ethics.*

People for the Ethical Treatment of Animals (PETA)
501 Front St., Norfolk, VA 23510
(757) 622-PETA • fax: (757) 622-0457
e-mail: peta@norfolk.infi.net • Web site: www.peta.org

An international animal rights organization, PETA is dedicated to establishing and protecting the rights of all animals. It focuses on four areas: factory farms, research laboratories, the fur trade, and the entertainment industry. PETA promotes public education, cruelty investigations, animal rescue, celebrity involvement, and legislative action. It produces numerous videos and publishes the children's magazine *Animal Times, Grrr!* as well as various fact sheets, brochures, flyers, and a weekly electronic newsletter.

Uncaged Campaigns
9 Bailey Ln., Sheffield S1 4EG, UK
+44 (0) 114 272 2220 • fax: +44 (0) 114 272 2225
e-mail: info@uncaged.co.uk • Web site: www.uncaged.co.uk

Uncaged Campaigns works to end vivisection and to ascribe moral and legal rights to animals. It is best known for winning a legal battle to release *Diaries of Despair*, the animal transplantation reports of Huntingdon Life Sciences, a commercial research company that Uncaged Campaigns accuses of breaching animal welfare practices. Members receive *Uncaged!*, its quarterly newsmagazine.

Zoocheck Canada
2646 St. Clair Ave. East, Toronto, ON M4B 3M1, Canada
(416) 285-1744 • fax: (416) 285-4670
e-mail: zoocheck@zoocheck.com • Web site: www.zoocheck.com

Zoocheck Canada aims to protect animal welfare through investigation, research, campaigns, and legal actions. Many of the news articles and reports on its Web site discuss animal welfare across the globe, including in the United States, Central and South America, and the United Kingdom. It produces videos, audiotapes, and reports about animal rights issues as well as a quarterly newsletter, *Natural Justice*, about animals and Canadian law.

Bibliography

Books

Jeremy Bentham — *The Principles of Morals and Legislation.* Amherst, NY: Prometheus Books, 1988.

Marion Stamp Dawkins — *Animal Suffering: The Science of Animal Welfare.* Boca Raton, FL: Chapman and Hall, 1980.

René Descartes — *Discourse on the Method*, in John Cottingham, Robert Stoothoff, and Dugald Murdoch, trans., *The Philosophical Writings of Descartes*, vol. 1. Cambridge: Cambridge University Press, 1985.

Gary L. Francione — *Animals, Property, and the Law.* Philadelphia: Temple University Press, 1995.

Gary L. Francione — *Introduction to Animal Rights: Your Child or the Dog?* Philadelphia: Temple University Press, 2000.

Jane Goodall — *The Ten Trusts: What We Must Do to Care for the Animals We Love.* San Francisco: HarperSanFrancisco, 2002.

C. Ray Greek and Jean Swingle Greek — *Sacred Cows and Golden Geese: The Human Cost of Experiments on Animals.* New York: Continuum, 2000.

Tom Regan and Peter Singer — *Animal Rights and Human Obligations.* 2nd ed. Englewood Cliffs, NJ: Prentice-Hall, 1989.

Matthew Scully — *Dominion: The Power of Man, the Suffering of Animals, and the Call to Mercy.* New York: St. Martin's Press, 2002.

Peter Singer — *Animal Liberation.* New York: Ecco Press, 2001.

Steven M. Wise — *Drawing the Line: Science and the Case for Animal Rights.* New York: Perseus, 2002.

Steven M. Wise — *Rattling the Cage: Toward Legal Rights for Animals*, Cambridge, MA: Perseus, 2000.

Periodicals

David Bjerklie, Dan Cray, and Dick Thompson — "Monkey Business," *Time*, January 22, 2001.

Bernice Bovenkerk, Frans W.A. Brom, and Babs J. van den Bergh — "Brave New Birds: The Use of 'Animal Integrity' in Animal Ethics," *Hastings Center Report*, January/February 2002.

Ron Epstein — "Genetic Engineering: A Buddhist Assessment," *Religion East and West*, June 2001.

Alix Fano — "Beastly Practice," *Ecologist*, May 2000.

Feed & Grain	"Standing Up to Animal Activists," April/May 2003.
Ralph Frammolino and James Bates	"Questions Raised About Group That Watches Out for Animals in Movies," *Los Angeles Times*, February 9, 2001.
Josh Getlin	"The Philosopher as Provocateur," *Los Angeles Times*, January 8, 2001.
Stanley M. Giannet	"The Human-Animal Divide: Interdisciplinary Ethical Reflections," *Journal of Evolutionary Psychology*, March 2003.
Brady R. Johnson	"Humane Rights," *January Magazine*, May 2000.
Adrian R. Morrison	"Personal Reflections on the 'Animal-Rights' Phenomenon," *Perspectives in Biology and Medicine*, Winter 2001.
Adrian R. Morrison	"Perverting Medical History in the Service of Animal Rights," *Perspectives in Biology and Medicine*, Autumn 2002.
David S. Oderberg	"The Illusion of Animal Rights," *Human Life Review*, Spring/Summer 2000.
Charles R. Pulver	"Will Animals Have Duties as Well as Rights?" *Wanderer*, October 28, 1999.
Michael Satchell	"Cruel and Usual," *U.S. News & World Report*, August 5, 2002.
Roger Scruton	"Urbanities: Animal Rights," *City Journal*, Summer 2000.
Kathryn Senior	"What Next After the First Transgenic Monkey?" *Lancet*, February 10, 2001.
Lisa Stansky	"Personhood for Bonzo?" *ABA Journal*, March 2000.
Solveig Torvik	"Will Chimps Make Chumps of Us in Court? Comes Now, Plaintiff Bonzo, in the Matter of *Bonzo v. Researchers*," *Seattle Post-Intelligencer*, April 30, 2002.
Stephen H. Webb	"Do All Good Dogs Go to Heaven?" *Books & Culture*, January/February 1999.
Clive D.L. Wynne	"The Soul of the Ape," *American Scientist*, March 2001.

Internet Sources

Heidi Bensen	"Interview with and About Koko," Free City Media, 2001. www.freecitymedia.com/BigKokoFrameSet.html.
Donald M. Bruce	"Should We Clone Animals?" Society, Religion, and Technology Project. www.srtp.org.uk/clonan3.htm.
Karen Davis	"The Experimental Use of Chickens and Other Birds in Biomedical and Agricultural Research," New England Anti-Vivisection Society, 2003. www.neavs.org.
Samantha Scott	"Assessment of the Physical and Psychological Wellbeing of Captive Wild and Exotic Animals," Zoocheck Canada. www.zoocheck.com/programs/zoocheck/psy.shtml.
Akiva Wolff	"A Jewish Perspective on Genetic Engineering," Center for Business Ethics. http://besr.org/library/engineering.html.

Index